Academic Writing
Practice
for
IELTS

Sam McCarter

About the author

Sam McCarter is co-author of *A book for IELTS* and *IELTS Reading Tests*, the author of *a book on writing, BPP English for PLAB* and *Nuffield Stress Tests for PLAB*. He has also co-authored several other publications and edited a range of health publications.

Sam is a lecturer in academic and medical English at Southwark College, where he organises IELTS courses for overseas doctors and other health personnel, and courses in medical English, including preparation for the OSCE component of the PLAB. He is also the creator and organiser of the Nuffield Self-access Language Project for Overseas Doctors and is a free-lance consultant in medical English, specialising in tropical medicine.

Future Publications by IntelliGene

IntelliGene will be publishing a major book on communication skills in medicine by Sam McCarter.

Preface

This book is for students preparing for the Writing Test in the Academic Module of the International English Language Testing System (IELTS), which is administered by the British Council, the University of Cambridge Local Examinations Syndicate (UCLES) and IELTS Australia.

The book is aimed at those candidates aiming to achieve a Band Score of 6 or more in the Academic Writing component in IELTS. The book contains six sections: *Section 1: Writing Practice for Task 1*; *Section 2: Writing Practice for Task 2*; *Section 3: Checking and Editing*; *Section 4: Practice Writing Tests; a Key*; and *an Appendix.*

All the graphs and the texts in this publication have been created by the author with the exception of the drawings in Section 1 Exercise 20.

The spelling in the book is British English.

All of the names in the publication are fictitious.

The book may be used as a supplement to *A Book for IELTS* by McCarter, Easton & Ash, *IELTS Reading Tests* by McCarter & Ash, *a book on writing* by Sam McCarter, or as a supplement to a course book, or for self-study.

So that you may repeat the exercises in this book, I would advise you to avoid marking the text.

Sam McCarter
June 2002

Introduction

The IELTS Academic Writing Section

The academic writing test in the IELTS exam lasts for 60 minutes.

The writing test contains two compulsory tasks, namely Task 1 and Task 2. In Task 1, you are asked to describe graphs, bar charts, pie charts and diagrams and in Task 2 you are given an essay title on a fairly general subject.

Task 1 assesses your ability to analyse data objectively without giving an opinion, whereas Task 2 usually requires a subjective piece of writing on a fairly general topic. In addition, it is worth noting that the exam is not testing knowledge of English language, but rather competence in using English. In other words, it is not testing memory. Awareness of this might help reduce some of the problems that many candidates have in the IELTS exam.

Word length and timing

In the exam, the minimum word limit for Task 1 is 150 words and you are advised to spend 20 minutes on this part of the test. For Task 2, the minimum word limit is 250 words, on which you are advised to spend 40 minutes. In both Tasks, there is no upper word limit.

Candidates frequently exceed the minimum amounts by a very wide margin, which creates several problems. Rather than concentrating on producing a good essay, candidates write beyond what is necessary, thinking that they will gain extra marks by writing more. This is usually not the case.

It is very important that you aim for the respective word limits, and perhaps write just a little more. You could write between 150 and 180 words for Task 1 and 250 and 300 for Task 2. While practising for the IELTS exam count the number of words you write per line and then work out how many lines you need to reach the 150/250 word limits. It may surprise you how little you have to write! You could draw a line to mark the word limits when you are writing your homework. This will help train you to keep to the limits and help you to focus on where you are going and what you are aiming for.

One important reason for writing just a little more than the word limit is to give yourself enough time to check your work for mistakes.

Task 1 or Task 2 first? Students frequently ask whether they should do Task 1 first or Task 2. This obviously depends on the individual. It is probably wise, however, to do the shorter task first as then you have the satisfaction of having completed one task.

Note that the value of the marks given to each Task is reflected in the time. Task 2 carries twice the number of marks as Task 1.

Note also that you cannot go below the word limits as this will probably affect your score band.

Aim of the publication

The aim of this book is to help make students flexible and competent in their writing so that they can write on any subject in the exam. There are many texts in the book, both essays and paragraphs, but rather than learn these by heart it is better if you can learn the mechanisms, so you can apply them in any situation.

Contents of the book

Section 1 contains 20 practice exercises for Task 1, which aim to make you more flexible when you are writing under pressure. Section 2 contains 25 exercises aimed at increasing your flexibility in writing for Task 2, focusing first on connections within the sentence, then between sentences and then in a paragraph. Section 3 contains a number of exercises on checking and editing. These are skills often neglected by candidates in the exam. Of the 20 minutes for Task 1 and the 40 minutes for task 2, you should be leave yourself two or three minutes in each task to check and edit your work. This is one reason why you should not write above 150/250 words.

The fourth section contains 10 practice writing tests, some of which have sample answers in the Key. In some cases, there are several sample answers for a task with different possible scores.

The last Section contains the Key and the Appendix contains an example of the answer sheet which is used in the exam.

Model and sample answers for the Writing Tests

Many students preparing for the IELTS examination learn model or sample answers by heart. They then go into the exam and either re-produce these answers, usually with lots of mistake, or they try to fit them into their essays. Some students learn, for example, a model about technology and then try to fit it into a similar, but different question in the exam; or do not even bother to try to fit it in, they just regurgitate it. Unfortunately, with the mistakes and the fact that the answer does not quite fit, candidates end up with a score lower than they are capable of achieving.

It is better to learn the mechanisms that will increase your competence and flexibility in writing and use the models or samples as standards against which you can measure your own writing.

CONTENTS | Page

Section 1

Writing Practice for Task 1

CONTENTS

Exercise 1: language for graphs

This exercise focuses on some basic language, which you need to describe graphs. Look at the graph below, which shows the number of visitors to Tabard Towers Theme Park each month last year. Following the graph, there are 15 statements about the data. Decide which sentences are true or false according to the diagram. More than one sentence may describe the same data.

Note that the sentences are not in any particular order and that they do not form a full text.

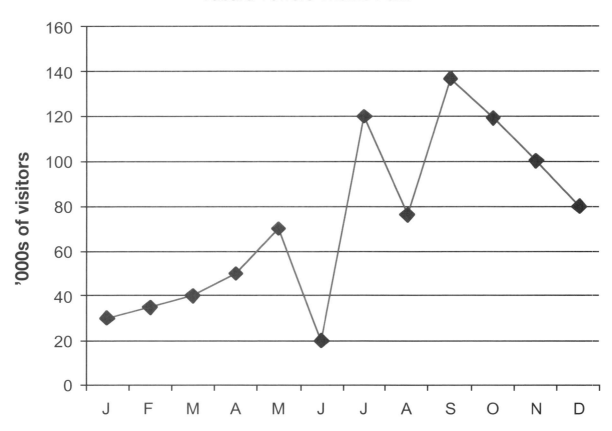

Tabard Towers Theme Park

1. In the last three months of the year, attendances were off their September peak, falling back by 30,000 visitors a month till the end of the year. ✓

2. During last year, the trend was obviously upwards.

3. Numbers picked up in June, rocketing by almost 400%.

4. There was a marked improvement in July with the number of visitors surging 500%.

5. From May through to September, the number of people visiting the theme park monthly rose by approximately 70%.

6. During the first four months, visitor numbers rose gradually.

7. The gradual rise in visitor numbers from 30,000 to approximately 45,000 in the first four months was followed by a sharper increase in May.

8. Between April and May, the increase in the number of visitors was at a much slower pace than in the previous three months.

9. It is clear that for most of the year, monthly attendances were above trend.

10. In July, the number of visitors shot up dramatically.

11. In July, there was a dramatic increase in visitor numbers to just short of 140,000 people, followed by a sudden decline in August.

12. In July, visitor numbers soared and then suddenly fell back again the following month.

13. August saw a sharp turnaround in attendances with numbers leaping from just under 80,000 to 140,000 people.

14. The period between May and September saw a steady growth in the number of visitors from 70,000 to 140,000.

15. Attendances at the theme park can be divided into three distinct periods: January to May, June to September and October to December.

Exercise 2: graph jumble

This exercise gives you more practice with basic language for graphs. Read the text below carefully. Then look at the 10 mini line graphs **A – J** and decide the sequence of the graphs. Note that there are 11 mini graphs in the sequence and that there is one mini graph which you will not use. You may use any graph more than once. **The first graph in the sequence is A.**

Text

The number of books sold was fairly steady over the first few weeks of the year with a slight rise to 200 per day. After that sales went up and down wildly, first doubling to 400 units, and subsequently falling back erratically again to 200 books. These fluctuations were followed by a period of stability as sales hovered around the 200 mark. Book purchases, however, proved very erratic again, but the trend was upward this time, reaching the 400 per day level. The number of books sold then plunged dramatically, hitting a low of 100, only to bounce back to 500 books a day. The recovery was short-lived, however, as sales fell back again to 200 around which they remained for a short time before climbing again, albeit fitfully to 400. Book sales then plummeted to a new low of 50 a day where they stabilised for a period before shooting up again to the 600 mark. This was followed by a sharp drop of approximately 80% in the number of books purchased.

A

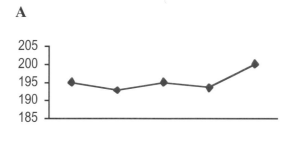

C

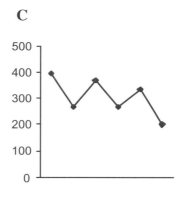

B

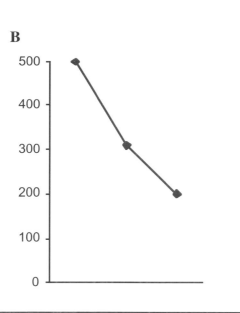

D

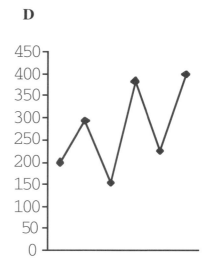

E

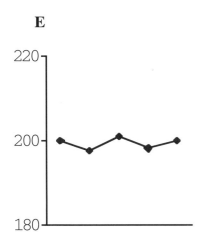

H

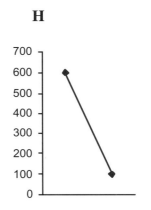

F

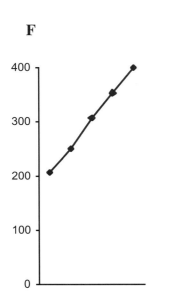

I

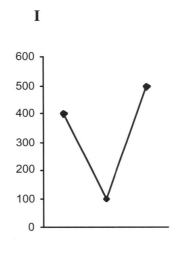

G

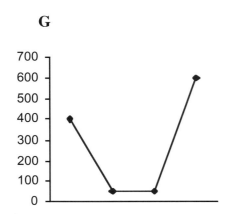

J

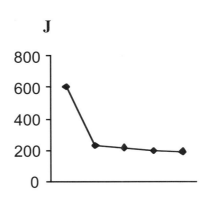

Exercise 3: missing data

In order to understand how to interpret data in a graph or chart, you need to be able to interact with the diagram. The exercise with the bar chart below will help you to do so.

The bar chart below shows the number of houses built per decade in two neighbouring towns, Farkletown and Newtown, during the last century. Look at the chart and then study the text which follows. Some information (A-S) has been left out of the text. Can you add it in the correct place? You may use each item once only.

Examples: 1. C 2. Q

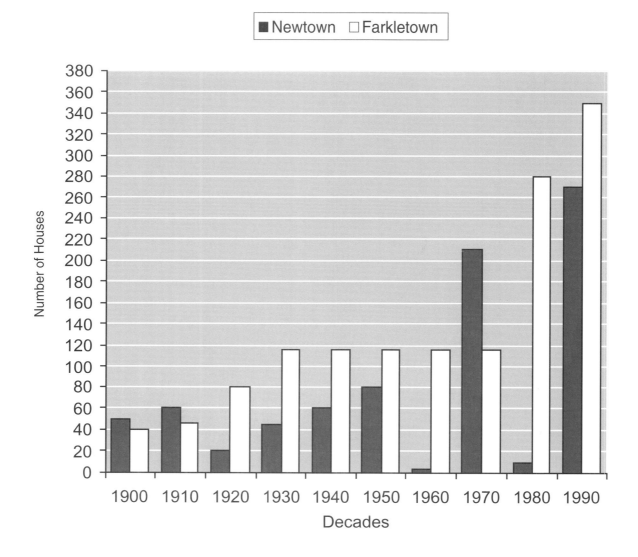

The number of houses built per decade in the towns of
Farkletown and Newtown over the last century

Missing information

A. 350 houses	H. three decades	O. only 10
B. only 20	I. erratic	P. 60s
C. 40 new houses	J. the 80s	Q. 10 years
D. the last two decades	K. over 200 houses	R. first two decades
E. over the next 40 years	L. practically to zero	S. a rise of more than 2600 %
F. 280	M. 120	
G. 70s	N. 1920s	

The bar chart shows the number of houses built per decade in two villages, Farkletown and Newtown, in the last century.

Overall, the number of houses that were erected in Farkletown exceeded the quantity constructed in Newtown. The trend for the former was decidedly upwards, with Farkletown experiencing a steady rise from _____1_____ in the first _____2_____ of the century, to just under 120 during the Thirties. _____3_____, new house construction in Farkletown remained constant at just under _____4_____. This is in sharp contrast to _____5_____ of the century when the number of houses that went up in Farkletown leapt, first to _____6_____ and then to _____7_____.

House building in Newtown, by comparison, was much more _____8_____. In the _____9_____ of the century, more houses were erected in Newtown than in Farkletown. During the _____10_____, however, construction declined to _____11_____. Over the next _____12_____, house numbers rose steadily, only to drop _____13_____ in the _____14_____. There was then a dramatic surge in the _____15_____ with _____16_____ being built. While _____17_____ saw house building in Newtown plummeting to _____18_____, in the 90s the number of new houses rocketed to 270, _____19_____ on the previous decade.

Exercise 4: interpretation questionnaire

Data, which are presented in a more complex form, tend to make students panic. However, when you realise that everything has a pattern, you can learn to control this panic. Look at the chart below and answer the questions, which follow.

The bar chart describes the results of a survey carried out on a sample of 1,000 adults aged 25+ to assess what makes modern life stressful.

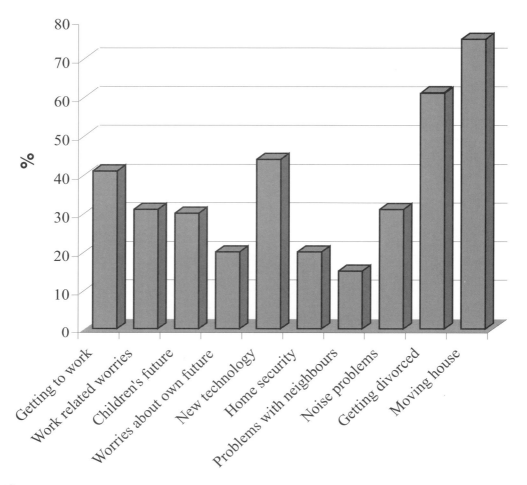

Factors that cause stress in modern day life

Questions

1. What makes the nature of the presentation of the data different from a graph?
2. What is the relationship between the horizontal and vertical axes?
3. Why does the scale only go up to 80 per cent?
4. What possible groups could you put the factors into?
5. Why would you use these groupings?
6. How would you compare *Moving house* with the other factors?
7. How would you compare *Problems with neighbours* with the other factors?
8. What other synonyms could you use for the word *factors*?

9.   Look at the following sentences:

  a)   Worries about own future *cited by just less than 20% of those sampled as a contributing factor to stress.*

  b)   *Thirty percent of the sample gave* Work related worries *a factor contributing to their stress.*

  c)   *According to the bar chart,* Getting to work *induced stress in 40 per cent of sampled.*

   What is missing in each sentence?

10.   What are the differences between the three sentences below?

  a)   *According to the bar chart, 30% of those questioned cite worries about the future of their children as a cause of stress.*

  b)   *According to the bar chart, worries about the future of their children caused stress to 30% of those questioned.*

  c)   *According to the bar chart, 30% of the sample suffered stress as a result of concerns about the future of their children.*

11.   Complete the following sentence:

   According to just under 30% of the sample, concerns about their children's future

   _____.

12.   When you describe bar charts like this, what makes them more difficult to describe than graphs?

Exercise 5: which month?

This exercise also aims to make you look carefully at data. The chart below shows the number of visitors each month to two exhibitions, namely an exhibition on Modern Sculpture and one on 20th Century Ephemera, over the past year. Below the chart, there are 11 sentences. In each sentence, the months have been omitted. Study the chart and add the appropriate months to the blank spaces.

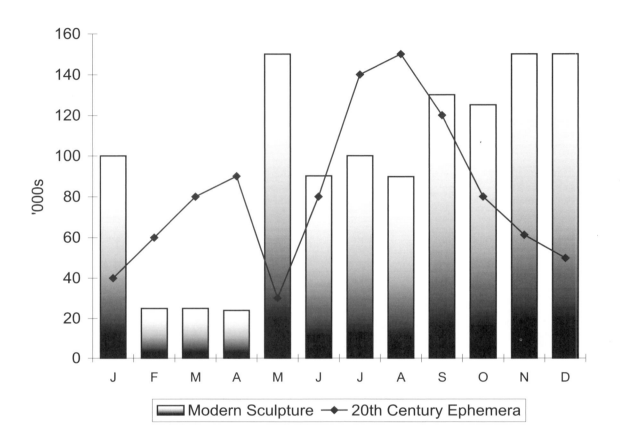

Visitors to two exhibitions

Sentences

1. While the number of visitors to the Modern Sculpture Exhibition fell in _____ by 75%, attendances at the Ephemera Exhibition rose 50% to 60,000 people.

2. Despite some poor figures from _____ to _____, the attendance trend at the Modern Sculpture Exhibition was upward.

3. Whereas, on the one hand, the number of visitors to the Sculpture Exhibition hovered around the 20 to 25,000 mark from _____ to _____, at the Ephemera Exhibition visitor numbers continued to rise.

4.   In _____, the number of people visiting the Ephemera Exhibition fell back considerably before surging to a new peak of 150,000 visitors in _____. At the Sculpture Exhibition, meanwhile, attendances, although erratic, hit a new peak of 150,000 in _____.

5.   Numbers at the Ephemera Exhibition, despite impressive attendances, ended the year not much above the _____ level.

6.   From _____ to _____, the number of people visiting the Ephemera Exhibition monthly increased by 125%, with attendances at the Modern Sculpture Exhibition during the same period plunging 75% in _____ and then remaining at around the 25,000 mark till _____.

7.   During _____, visitor numbers surged at the Modern Sculpture Exhibition with a 500% leap corresponding with a 66% drop in attendances at the Ephemera Exhibition.

8.   _____ attendances at the Modern Sculpture Exhibition fell back dramatically with a 40% fall, but by contrast the Ephemera Exhibition witnessed a dramatic turnaround which lasted through to _____, when visitor numbers hit a peak of 150,000.

9.   In the last four months of the year attendances at the Ephemera Exhibition fell off substantially, whereas the number of people coming to visit the Modern Sculpture Exhibition, while erratic, climbed to their _____ peak in _____ and remained there in _____.

10.   While the visitor numbers at the Ephemera Exhibition plunged by two thirds, from 150,000 to 50,000, between _____ and _____ , the number of visitors to the Modern Sculpture exhibition rose erratically to more than 150,000.

11.   Until _____, the trend for the 20th Century Exhibition was upward, but thereafter visitor numbers fell steeply.

Exercise 6: comparison - no trends

The data in this exercise are presented in a way which is more like Exercise 4 than the other exercises: there are no dates and no progression. and no trends. The chart shows the results of a survey in percentage terms comparing the participation in various home activities among young people aged 11 to 16 in four countries.

Study the chart and match the items in the left-hand column (1-11), which are in the correct order, with those on the right (A-K), which are jumbled, in order to create a text. The first two items (1 and J), which continue the opening sentence, are given to you in bold. The closing part of the text is also given after the two columns.

Home activities among young people

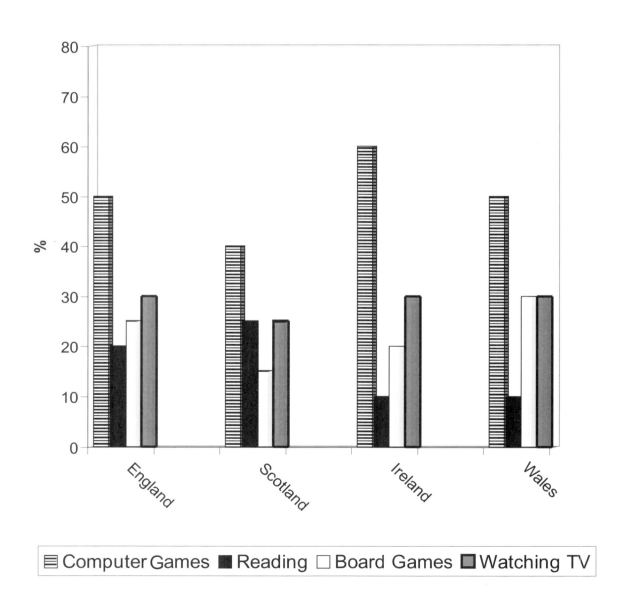

Jumbled text

The bar chart shows the results of a survey on the number of young people aged 11 – 16 in ...

1. **England, Scotland, Ireland and Wales who**

2. Computer Games, Reading, Watching TV

3. As can be seen clearly, the most striking feature of the chart is that in all

4. In England, for example, more young people

5. than any other activity with 20% of young people participating in Reading,

6. A similar pattern is repeated in Ireland,

7. playing Computer Games is higher than

8. at 10%, Board Games at 20% and Watching

9. Scotland as well with a 40 per cent participation rate, but, unlike

10. is greater at 25% as opposed to 20% and 10%

11. come out first at 50%, but

A. England and Ireland, the percentage involved in Reading

B. in England at 60% with Reading the lowest

C. TV at 30%. Computer Games come top in

D. four countries playing Computer Games has the highest participation rate.

E. (50% of the sample) play Computer Games

F. and Board Games.

G. involvement in Reading was the lowest of the

H. 25% in Board Games and 30% in Watching TV.

I. but here the percentage of those

J. **take part in four indoor activities, namely:**

K. respectively. In Wales, Computing Games

... four countries at under 10% with Watching TV and Board Games equal at 30%.

Exercise 7: looking at data with more complex presentation

The data in this exercise are presented in a more complex form. However, as in the other exercises, there are patterns. Look at the figure below and answer the questions, which follow.

The graph below shows the writing activity of four writers throughout their lifetime. The vertical scale shows their writing activity and the horizontal scale shows their age. Any writing activity above 50 led to publication.

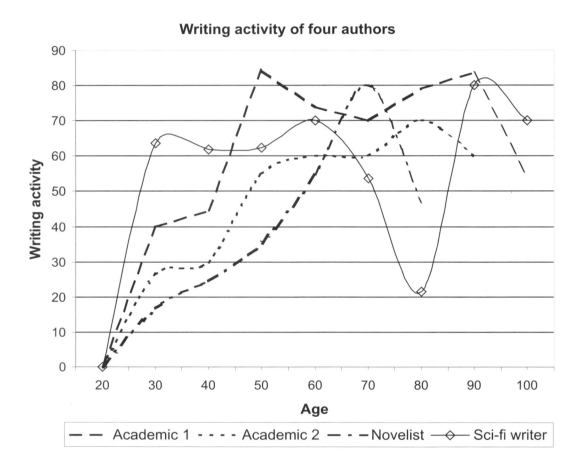

Questions

1. At what age did the four writers start writing?
2. When did the sci-fi writer first have his work published?
3. What age was the sci-fi writer when he died?
4. During which periods of his life did the sci-fi writer publish his work?
5. When did Academic 1 have his first work published?
6. What did Academics 1 and 2 have in common?
7. Which writer had the shortest publishing period?
8. What did Academic 1 have in common with the sci-fi writer?
9. What four factors distinguished the novelist from the other three writers?
10. What possible groups could you put the four writers into?
11. Why would you use these groupings?

Exercise 8: label the diagram

The graph, pie charts and exercise below give you more practice with looking at data. The graph shows the daily sales figures in '000s of euros for three shopping complexes in different parts of the country for the first 12 days of January 2002. The shopping complexes are called TewkesMart, ThamesMart and FineMart. Below the graph is a pie chart showing the sales in percentage terms in various departments in one of the complexes.

Following the charts, there is a text, which describes the data in the diagrams. Use the text to label the charts. You may write your answers in the table (**A – O**) below.

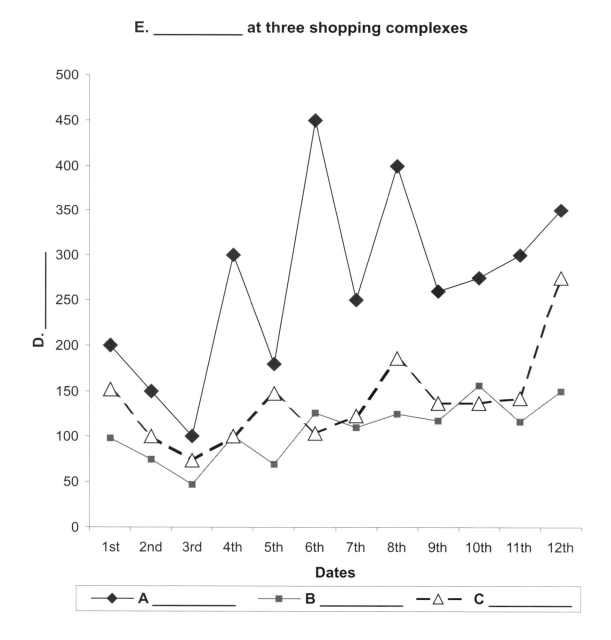

E. _____ at three shopping complexes

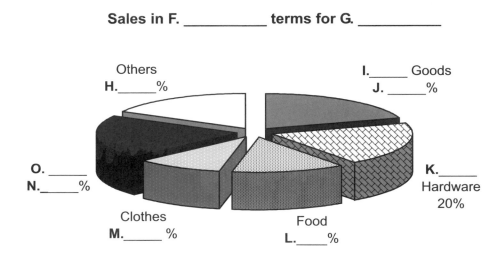

Sales in F. _____ terms for G. _____

Others
H._____%

I._____ Goods
J. _____%

O. _____
N._____%

K._____
Hardware
20%

Clothes
M._____%

Food
L.____%

Text

Between 1st and 3rd January, sales in each of the three complexes fell back by approximately fifty per cent. There was, however, a marked improvement on the 4th for ThamesMart, where the figure rose to 300,000 euros. This advance was followed by five days of quite wild fluctuations with takings falling to just over 250,000 euros on the 9th. ThamesMart, however, still maintained its lead, finishing the period at 350,000 euros. The sales figures for both TewkesMart and FineMart were also volatile with the former rising from monthly sales of 150,000 euros to about 275,000 at the end of the twelve days. FineMart, by contrast, ended only 50,000 up at 150,000 on 12th January.

The pie chart shows the sales figures in percentage terms for TewkesMart over the period. Electrical Goods, Computer Hardware and Toys made up the bulk of the sales with each accounting for 20 per cent of the total. Food represented 13% and Clothes came in at 10 per cent. As for Others, they represented 17 per cent of the total.

Clearly, the trends for the daily sales in all three shopping complexes were upward over the twelve-day period, albeit by varying degrees.

Complete the table below

A _____	G _____	L _____
B _____	H _____	M _____
C _____	I _____	N _____
E _____	J _____	O _____
F _____	K _____	

Exercise 9: following the chart

This exercise is the reverse of the previous one. The chart below shows the sales figures in '000s of euros for three shopping complexes, FinGroup Ltd, Man Ltd and Bluebird Ltd, in different parts of the country each month last year.

Below the diagram there is a text, which describes the data. Look at the chart and read the text through carefully. You can see that in the text most of the names relating to the three complexes have been omitted. Use the chart to complete the text.

For example the answer to number 1 is *FinGroup Ltd*.

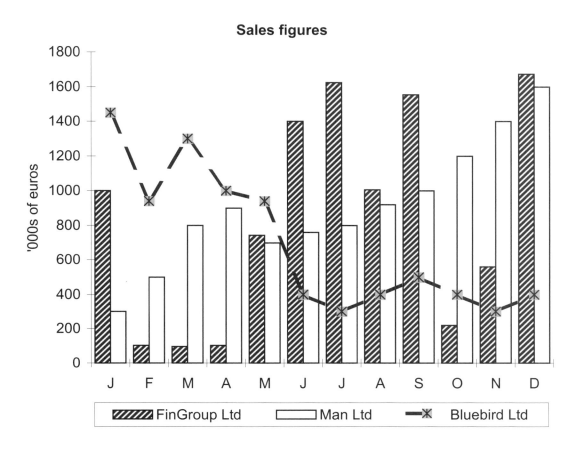

Sales figures

The sales trends in the three shopping complexes followed very different patterns over the past year with _____1_____ and _____2_____ on an upward trend and _____3_____ in decline. Whereas at _____4_____ monthly takings rose over the period by 433%, from approximately 300,000 euros in January to just under 1.6 million euros in December, those at _____5_____ climbed only 70% to over 1.5 million euros. For _____6_____, the year began with sales of one million euros, but then they fell back to just over 100,000 euros in each of the next three months. In May, sales figures at _____7_____ picked up, exceeding _____8_____, but still well below _____9_____.

In June, _____10_____, with a figure of 1.4 million euros, and _____11_____, with 750,000 euros, overtook _____12_____ for the first time. For the rest of the year _____13_____'s sales climbed steadily, whereas at _____14_____ the amount of money taken proved rather erratic. Excluding October and November, however, _____15_____'s sales outstripped those of _____16_____ for most of the period. Bluebird Ltd continued its decline, ending the year with sales of 400,000 in December.

Exercise 10: building flexibility

This exercise focuses on increasing your flexibility in using the language for graphs. Look at the chart below about the number of computers sold at VH Warehouse Ltd over a three year period and the sentences, which follow.

Rewrite each sentence using the words given. Note that there may be more than one way of rewriting the sentences.

Look at the following example:

> *In the fourth quarter of 1999, sales dropped to 6,000 computers.*
> *_____ drop _____.*
> *In the fourth quarter of 1999, there was a drop in sales to 6,000 computers.*

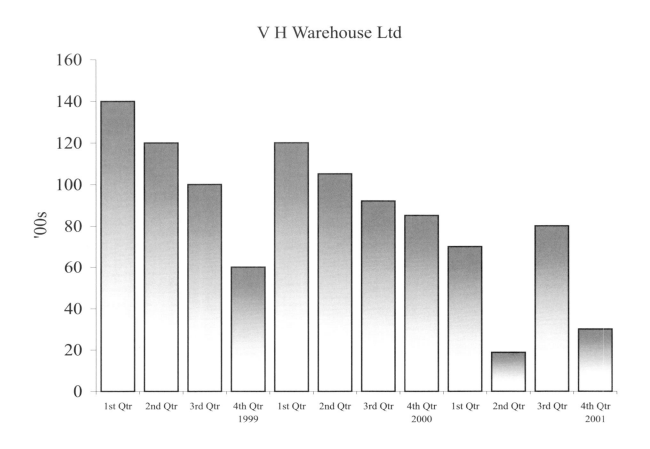

V H Warehouse Ltd

1.   In 2001, personal computer sales fluctuated wildly at V H Warehouse Ltd.

      In 2001, _____ wild _____.

2.   During the three-year period, the trend was obviously downward.

       During the three-year period, there _____.

3.   Sales picked up again in the first quarter of 2000, rocketing by more than 100%.

      _____, _____ rocketed by more than 100%.

4. Computer sales improved markedly in the first quarter of 2000 when they surged more than 100%.

    There _____ with _____.

5. From the first quarter of 2000 through to the first quarter of 2001, the number of computers sold quarterly fell by at least 1,000.

    From the first quarter of 2000 through to the first quarter of 2001, _____ a fall

    _____.

6. The decline in PC sales during the first three quarters of 1999 was gradual.

    _____ declined _____.

7. The gradual fall in quarterly computer sales from 14,000 to approximately 6,000 in the first four quarters was followed by a sharp increase in the first quarter of 2000 to 12,000.

    After falling _____.

8. Between the first quarter of 2000 through to the first quarter of 2001, the decrease in sales was at a much slower pace than in 1999.

    Between the first quarter of 2000 through to the first quarter of 2001, _____ decreased

    _____.

9. Generally speaking, over the period as a whole, the decrease in computer purchases was significant.

    Generally speaking, over the year as a whole, there _____.

10. In the third quarter of 2001, the volume of sales jumped dramatically.

    In the third quarter of 2001, there _____.

11. In the second quarter of 2001, there was a dramatic decline in computer sales to under 2,000 machines, followed by a sudden leap to 8,000 in the third quarter.

    Declining _____ in the second quarter of 2000, _____.

12. In the first quarter of 2000, purchases soared and then fell back again the following month.

    After _____, _____.

Exercise 11: projection in the past

The chart below shows the number of passengers on a new ferry link in its first year of operation and the estimated number of passengers over the same period. You can see that the chart is incomplete. Read the text following the chart and complete the line graph and bar chart.

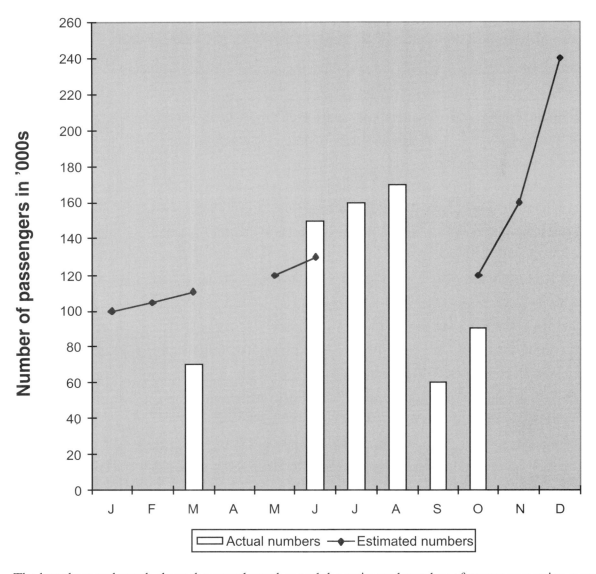

The bar chart and graph show the actual number and the estimated number of passengers using a new ferry link during its first year of operation.

Generally speaking, except for three months in the middle of the year, namely, June to August inclusive, the actual number of passengers fell short of projections. While it was forecast that passenger numbers would rise gradually from 100,000 in January to approximately 115,000 in April, the actual number was 90,000 at the beginning of the year falling in equal steps to 60,000 in April. In May, actual numbers rose to meet expectations.

From June to August, the actual number of passengers, exceeded expectations, hitting a peak of 170,000 in August itself and overshooting the target by 20,000 in each of the three months. In September, numbers declined, plunging sharply to 60,000, half the figure of 120,000 estimated for the month.

In the last three months of the year, actual numbers were a quarter below projection, but by December they had exceeded the August peak to stand at 180,000 passengers.

Exercise 12: compare and contrast

The table and exercise below give you more practice with the language of comparing and contrasting. The table shows the average number of telephone calls received in two sections of an office in one working day from 08.00 until 17.00 hours. The calls were rounded up to multiples of 10 (/////////). After the table there is a pie chart, showing the staffing ratio of the two sections.

Study the data below carefully.

Time	Section A	Section B
8.00		///////// ///////// /////////
8.30	///////// /////////	/////////
9.00	/////////	///////// ///////// /////////
9.30	/////////	///////// /////////
10.00	///////// /////////	///////// /////////
10.30	/////////	///////// /////////
11.00	///////// /////////	///////// /////////
11.30	///////// /////////	///////// /////////
12.00	///////// /////////	///////// /////////
12.30	/////////	Office closed
13.00	///////// ///////// /////////	///////// ///////// /////////
13.30	/////////	///////// ///////// /////////
14.00	///////// /////////	///////// ///////// /////////
14.30	/////////	///////// /////////
15.00	/////////	///////// /////////
15.30	/////////	/////////
16.00	/////////	/////////
16.30		/////////
Total	240	350

Now read the text below. You can see that the verbs are missing and that there are 21 blank spaces. Put the verbs from the list on the right into the appropriate place. You may use each item from the verb list only once. Please note that there are more blank spaces than there are verbs so you will have to leave some of the spaces empty. Remember to try to avoid repeating words close to each other.

Please note that the verbs include verbs in the -ing form and past participles.

Percentage of total staff

45%   55%

■ Section A   □ Section B

Two of the verbs have been inserted as examples

Text	Verbs

Text

The table **shows** the average number of telephone calls **received** in two sections of an office in one working day from 08.00 until 17.00 hours. The calls _____1_____ to multiples of 10 (//////////). The pie chart _____2_____ the staffing ratio of the two sections.

Despite _____3____ only 45% of the total staff _____4_____ as against 55% for Section A, Section B _____5_____ more in-coming calls overall _____6_____ at 350 per day _____7_____ in comparison to 240 for the other section. For example, while the average number of calls _____8_____ by Section A _____9_____ zero in the first half-hour _____10_____ between 8 and 8.30 am, Section B _____11_____ on average 30 calls. Moreover, Section B _____12_____ its 100th call by 10.30, whereas _____13_____ this point _____14_____ in Section A until after 11.30.

The only times _____15_____ during the day that the number of in-coming calls _____16_____ by Section A _____17_____ those _____18_____ with by Section B _____19_____ between 8.30 and 9 am and 12.30 and 13.00. By contrast, Section B ____20_____ more calls than Section A in nine of the periods, in spite of ____21_____ for half an hour between 12.30 and 13.00.

Verbs

i.   receives
ii.   has recorded
iii.   is not reached
iv.   is
v.   received
vi.   exceeds
vii.   is
viii.   are rounded up
ix.   illustrates
x.   making up
xi.   handles
xii.   taken
xiii.   takes
xiv.   being closed
xv.   taken
xvi.   shows
xvii.   dealt

Exercise 13: pie charts

The pie charts below show the market share over a decade, of a new washing machine introduced by Dyton in 1990. The bar chart shows the results of a survey on whether customers would consider buying the new Dyton washing machine over the same period

Market share in 1990

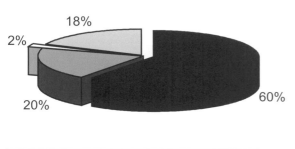

18%

2%

60%

20%

■ MMC Ltd   ■ Corr Ltd
□ Dyton   □ Obecalp

Market share in 1995

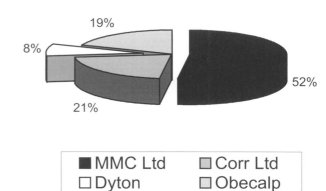

19%

8%

52%

21%

■ MMC Ltd   ■ Corr Ltd
□ Dyton   □ Obecalp

Popularity Survey

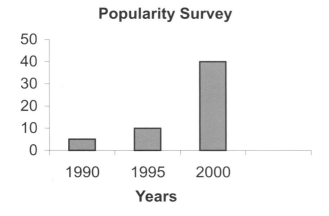

50
40
30
20
10
0

1990   1995   2000

Years

Market share in 2000

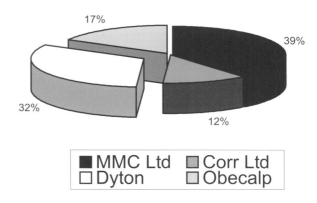

17%

39%

32%

12%

■ MMC Ltd   ■ Corr Ltd
□ Dyton   □ Obecalp

Look at the description of the data below. You can see that there are some words and phrases missing. Add words and phrases from the list following the text to complete the description.

The pie charts show the market share of washing machines four companies over the period 1990 to 2000 and the results of a survey customers would consider buying the new Dyton washing machine over the same period.

During the first year of sales of the new Dyton machine in 1990, its market share 2 percent 60 percent for the MMC product, 20 for the Corr washing machine and 18 for Obecalp. In 1995, however, MMC Ltd its three other competitors. While Corr Ltd and Obecalp Ltd both increased their market share by one percentage point each in 1995, Dyton Ltd 8% of the market, 300%.

In 2000, Dyton's market share had increased to 32% its three main competitors with MMC Ltd, Obecalp Ltd and Corr Ltd falling to 39 percent, 17 percent and 12 percent.

The bar chart shows that the Dyton machine its popularity rating in each year, rising from 5 in 1995 to 40 percent in the year 2000.

It is clear from the data that sales of the Dyton washing machine were on the increase over the period.

Word and phrase list

1. made by	5. exceeded	10. respectively
2. on whether	6. at the expense of	11. that of
3. lost ground to	7. captured	
4. stood at	8. a rise of	
	9. as opposed to	

Exercise 14: language jigsaw

The bar chart below shows the results of a survey on the general public's attitude towards different professions. After the chart, there is a sample text, which has been broken up into sections A – R in paragraph 1 and sections S – Y in paragraph 2. The parts of text have then been jumbled. The beginning of the text has been done for you as an example.

Put the jumbled items in the correct order to create the text. The punctuation and the grammar will help you.

Popularity of different professions

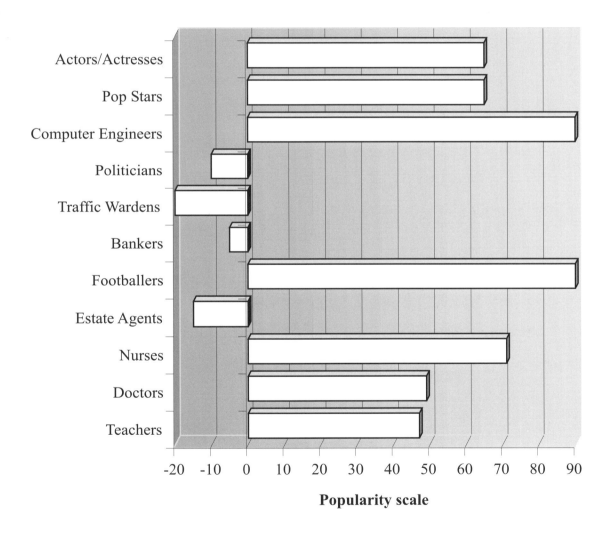

Popularity scale

Paragraph 1

The bar chart shows the result of a survey on the general public's ...

A. followed closely

B. each with a score of 90.

C. The second most popular occupation

D. and those which have a negative rating.

E. attitude towards different professions.

F. into two categories,

G. Footballers and Computer Engineers,

H. The first group is the

I. The jobs can be divided

J. by Actors/Actresses and Pop Stars,

K. Doctors are slightly more popular than

L. Teachers at 48 and 45% respectively,

M. among which the two most popular are

N. is Nurses with 70,

O. who each have a positive rating

P. namely those which have a positive

Q. of 65.

R. larger of the two with seven occupations,

... making Teachers the least popular occupation in this group.

Paragraph 2

In the negative category, which is comprised of Politicians, Traffic Wardens, Bankers and Estate Agents, ...

S. Estate Agents are rated more

T. with a score of minus 20.

U. Traffic Wardens are the most

V. unpopular

W. whereas Bankers, by contrast, are the least

X. unpopular, with a score of minus 5.

Y   unpopular than Politicians at minus 15 and 10 respectively,

Overall, there are more professions that are regarded posivitely than negatively.

Exercise 15: prediction choices

This exercise gives you practice with the future and avoiding repetition. Study the chart below, which shows two forecasts about the yearly growth in the number of people in Reamington, a new dormitory town.

Forecasts for population growth

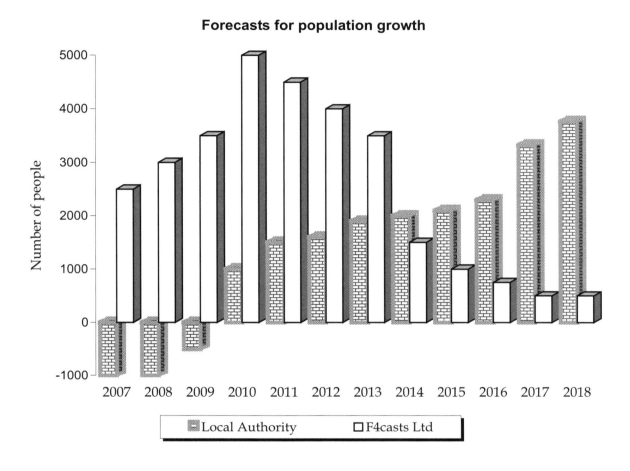

Below is the first sentence of a description of the bar chart.

> The chart shows two predictions of population growth in the dormitory town of Reamington, one by the local authority and the other by an independent firm of forecasters, called F4casts Ltd.

Choose an alternative to continue the text at each stage below. As you make your choices, try to avoid repetition. Remember repetition includes using the same structures and vocabulary close together and phrases in the same position, especially at the beginning of sentences.

The first answer is marked for you in italics. Why is it the best answer?

1. A *According to the former, from 2007 until 2009 inclusive,*
   B According to the predictions of the local authority, from 2007 up to and including 2009,
   C From 2007 until 2009, the prediction is that
   D The former shows that

2. A the town is expected to experience negative population growth
   B Reamington will lose people
   C numbers will drop down
   D Reamington's population is in for a fall

3. A with a decline of 1000 people in 2007 and again in 2008
   B and the population is expected to experience a decline by 1000 people in 2007 and in 2008
   C and there is expected to be negative growth in the population of 1000 people in 2007 and 2008
   D and the decline is expected to be 1000 people in 2007 and in 2008

4. A and after that there will be a tinier decline of 500 people in 2009.
   B and after that the decline will be smaller at 500 people in 2009.
   C and a drop of 500 people in 2009.
   D followed by a smaller drop of 500 in 2009.

5. A From 2010, the prediction is that
   B It is forecast that, from 2010 onwards,
   C From 2010 onwards, there is a prediction that
   D It is also expected that

6. A the number of people will grow up
   B population growth will enter positive territory
   C things will go up
   D the growth trend will be on the way up

7. A and then it will rise from approximately 1000 people in 2010 to almost 4000 in the year 2018.
   B quadrupling to almost 4000 people in the year 2018 from 1,000 in 2010.
   C with a rise of approximately 1000 people in 2010 to almost 4000 in the year 2018.
   D and it is forecast that the rise will be approximately 1000 people in 2010 to almost 4000 by the year 2018.

8. A F4casts Ltd, by contrast, predict
   B F4casts Ltd, by contrast, have forecast
   C F4casts Ltd, on the contrary, say
   D As regards F4casts Ltd, their prediction is

9. A the people of Reamington will expand
   B an expansion in the population of Reamington
   C the population growth of Reamington will be expanding
   D the population of Reamington will be on the up

10. A rising by 2500 people in 2007,
    B initially at the speed of 2500 people in 2007,
    C going up by 2500 people in 2007,
    D by 2500 people in 2007,

11. A increasing to 5000 in the year 2010.
    B rising to 5000 in 2010.
    C after which it will increase to 5000 in the year 2010.
    D and then there will be a rise to 5000 in the year 2010.

12. A However, after that Reamington's growth will slow down,
    B Thereafter, however, the population growth in Reamington is anticipated to be slower,
    C Thereafter, however, growth is anticipated to slacken a bit,
    D However, the population is predicted to slow up,

13. A to drop in stages to 500 people by the year 2018.
    B with drops in stages to 500 people by the year 2018.
    C with droppings in stages to 500 people by the year 2018.
    D and fall in stages to 500 people by the year 2018.

Exercise 16: something wrong with the prediction

This exercise also looks at talking about the future. Study the bar chart below, which shows the profits for three companies for next year.

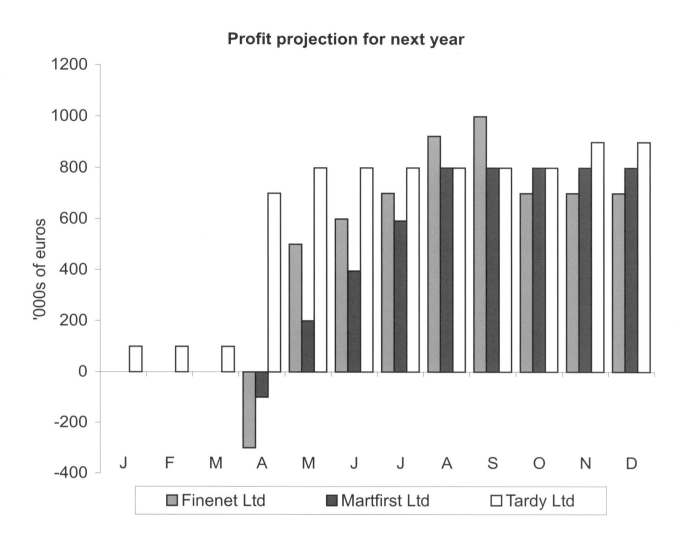

Profit projection for next year

Text

Now look at the text below. There is something wrong with the description - none of the mistakes are connected with grammar or spelling, but with vocabulary and data. How many can you find? The first one is the word *presumed* in line 1. It is not suitable here – predicted, perhaps?

The bar chart shows the presumed profits for next year in thousands of dollars for three companies, two of which will not start trading until May.

Tardy's profits are forecast to come in at the 200,000 level in January and are then expected to remain there until May, following which it is estimated that they will shoot up twofold in one month, to 700,000 euros in June. After a modest rise in May to 800,000 euros, profits are set to remain erratic for the rest of the year.

Similarly, it is projected that the profit for Martfirst will operate at a loss of 100,000 euros in the first month of trade in January. Thereafter, however, there is anticipated to be a steady increase in profits, which will climb at the rate of 100,000 euros per month until they reach 800,000 euros in August. Profits will then remain steady for the rest of the year.

As regards Finenet Ltd, a loss of 300,000 euros is expected in its first month of trading, but then from May to October, profits will climb quickly to 1 million euros, before falling back considerably in the subsequent three months.

As can be seen, the overall trends for the three companies are upward.

Exercise 17: guided writing

The bar chart below shows the results of '360-degree testing' as part of a performance assessment carried out by colleagues and subordinates of four managers. Those who participated in the assessment were asked to rate the performance of the four managers on a percentage scale. Below the chart is a model answer.

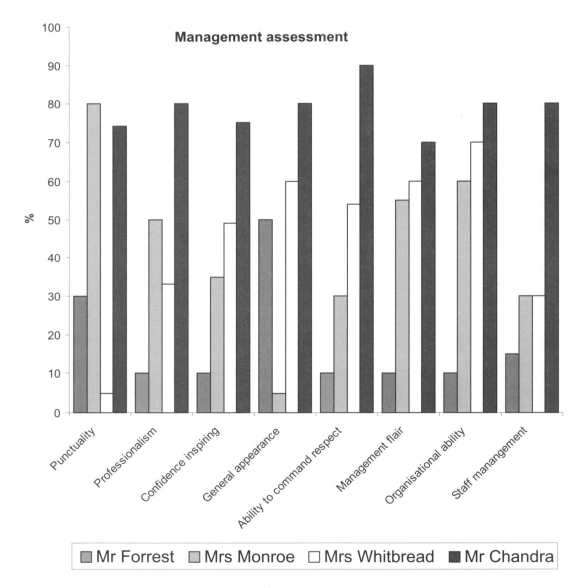

Model answer

Study the chart as quickly as you can and add the relevant percentages to the model below.

The bar chart shows the results of a performance assessment by the colleagues and subordinates of four managers. In the assessment, the performance of the four managers was rated on a percentage scale.

One of the most striking features of the chart is the ratings scored by Mr Chandra, who consistently achieved _____(1)_____ or above in all categories with the highest being the *Ability to command respect* at _____(2)_____ and the lowest, *Management flair*, at _____(3)_____. Mr Chandra also came out top in seven out of the eight categories

Mr Forrest, however, was at the opposite end of the scale. Out of the eight categories, he scored only _____(4)_____ in five, managing to gain higher ratings in only three categories, of which the top was _____(5)_____ for *General appearance*. For the other two, *Punctuality* and *Staff management*, Mr Forrest gained _____(6)_____ and _____(7)_____ respectively.

Of the other two managers, Mrs Monroe's scores ranged from _____(8)_____, her highest rating, for *Punctuality* to _____(9)_____ for *General Appearance*, the lowest of all four managers in this category. Likewise, Mrs Whitbread scored in the range of _____(10)_____ for *Organisational ability* to _____(11)_____ for *Staff management*.

Guided writing

Now without looking at the model, complete in your own words the text below and then compare it with the KEY.

_____(1)_____ the results of a performance assessment by the colleagues and subordinates of four managers. In the assessment, the performance of the four managers was _____(2)_____.

_____(3)_____ of the chart is the ratings scored by Mr Chandra, who consistently achieved 70% or above in all categories _____(4)_____ being the *Ability to command respect* at 90% and the lowest, *Management flair*, at 70%. Mr Chandra _____(5)_____ in seven out of the eight categories

Mr Forrest, however, was at the _____(6)_____. _____(7)_____ the eight categories, he scored only 10% in five, _____(8)_____ higher ratings in only three categories, of which the top was 50% for *General appearance*. For the other two, *Punctuality* and *Staff management*, Mr Forrest _____(9)_____ 30% and 15%, _____(10)_____.

Of the other two managers, Mrs Monroe's scores _____(11)_____ from 80%, her highest rating, for *Punctuality* to 5% for *General Appearance*, the lowest of all four managers in this category. _____(12)_____, Mrs Whitbread scored in the range of 70% for *Organisational ability* to 30% for *Staff management*.

Exercise 18: describe the changes

This exercise gives you practice with describing changes and with flexibility in your language, but this time with diagrams rather than charts. Diagram A below shows Sorrel Cottage and the surrounding land in 1980. Diagram B shows the changes that took place from 1980 to 2002 followed by a Key.

Diagram A: Sorrel Cottage and Garden 1980

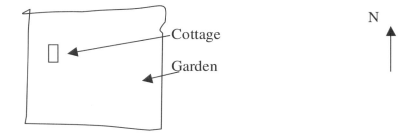

Diagram B: Sorrel Cottage and Garden 2002

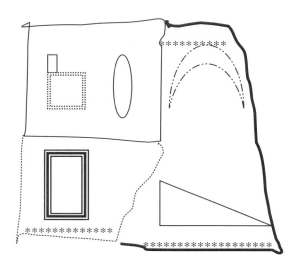

Key

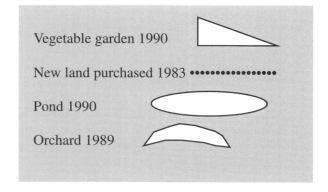

Vegetable garden 1990	New land purchased 1985
New land purchased 1983	Trees 1996 *************
Pond 1990	Addition to house 1986-1988
Orchard 1989	Open air swimming pool 2000-2001

Model text

Diagrams A and B show the changes that took place at Sorrel Cottage between 1980 and 2002. The garden was considerably enlarged by the purchase of two plots of land: one adjacent to the southern border, which was bought in 1983 and which is almost equal in size to the original garden; and the other plot on the eastern border, which was bought in 1985, and which effectively doubled the area of the garden again.

Between 1986 and 1988, an extension was built on to the southern side of the cottage and in the following year an orchard was planted in the northern part of the land acquired in 1985. The year 1990 saw two additions to the property: a pond in the original garden and a vegetable garden on the other side of the garden from the orchard. A line of trees was planted along the southern edge of the garden and another one above the orchard in 1996.

Between 2000 and 2001, an open-air swimming pool was built in the land purchased in 1983.

Textual transformation

Now use the text above to help you complete the text below, while making as few changes as possible to the original text. For example, for number 1 below the answer is: *of changes took place.*

According to diagrams A and B, a number _____(1)_____ at Sorrel Cottage between 1980 and 2002. The purchase of two _____(2)_____. The one _____(3)_____ in 1983 and _____(4)_____ in size the original garden. Then in the year 1985 the area covered by the garden _____(5)_____ acquisition _____(6)_____ on the eastern border.

Between 1986 and 1988, the cottage _____(7)_____ and the following year saw the _____(8)_____ in the northern part of the land acquired in 1985. A pond was _____(9)_____ in 1990 and in the same year _____(10)_____ on the other side of the garden from the orchard. In 1996, two _____(11)_____, one along the southern edge of the garden and the other above the orchard.

Between 2000 and 2001, an open-air swimming pool was built in the land purchased in 1983.

Exercise 19: a table

Look at the table below, which shows the percentage participation of women in senior management in three companies between 1960 and the year 2000. You can see that some of the data are missing. Read the description, which follows the table, and fill in the missing information.

	MACROHARD LTD	___A___	___B___
	%	%	%
_C_	___D___	8	___I___
1965	___E___	10	13
1970	13	12	___J___
1975	26	14	21
1985	___F___	___H___	19
2000	___G___	45	25

The table shows the percentage of women in senior management positions in three companies from 1960 to 2000.

While more women were in senior positions at Eastman Ltd than the other two companies in 1960 at 15 %, the trend was fairly erratic with a 2% drop to 13% in 1965, followed by a rise of 1% five years later. In 1975, women held 7% more top management jobs than in 1970. After a slight drop back to 19% in 1985, by 2000 25% of top posts were filled by women.

By contrast, at Macrohard Ltd women fared much better. In 1960, 2% of senior posts were occupied by women with no change five years on. By 1970, the figure had increased to 13%, doubling to 26 per cent in 1975. Ten years afterwards, there was a 6% increase in female senior management jobs with a near twofold jump in 2000 to stand at 63%, the highest for the three companies.

The situation was less remarkable at Barnes Ltd than the other two firms except for the year 2000. In 1960, the percentage of senior posts held by women was 8% climbing at the rate of 2% in each subsequent period until 1985, after which it leapt to 45%

From the data, it is clear that women dominated senior posts at Macrohard by 2000.

Exercise 20: a life-cycle

Look at the text and the jumbled pictures (A-J) below about the life-cycle of a ladybird. In the text, there are seven places where you have to choose one correct alternative to continue the text. Once you have done this, put the jumbled pictures in the order they are mentioned in the text. The first picture is J.

The diagrams ...

1. (A) show the life cycle of a ladybird from the time of mating	(B) lists the life cycle of a ladybird from the time of mating	(C) shows life cycle of insects

through to adulthood.

2. (A) At the beginning of the cycle, the ladybirds mate for	(B) In the beginning of the life-cycle, ladybirds mated for	(C) In the life cycle's beginning, ladybirds mate for

approximately two hours. The female ladybird ...

3. (A) as a result lays up to a dozen eggs on a nettle leaf and after all that leaves the little eggs to hatch on their own.	(B) consequently lays up to a dozen eggs on a nettle leaf and then left the eggs to come out on their own.	(C) then lays up to a dozen eggs on a nettle leaf before leaving them to hatch on their own.

About a week after the ladybird has laid its eggs, depending on the temperature they become darker and larvae hatch.

4. (A) The bodies of the new-born larvae darken. They eat its own egg shells.	(B) The bodies of the new-born larvae darken and they eat their own eggshells.	(C) Bodies of new-born larvae darken and eats own egg shells.

The larvae feed on aphids, which are their favourite prey. After a period of …

5. (A) three to six weeks, during this time the ladybird larvae grow,

(B) three to six weeks, during this time insect larvae grow,

(C) three to six weeks, during which time the ladybird larvae grow,

the fully-grown larvae turns into pupae.

6. (A) A week or two later, ladybird emerges out of a pupa

(B) A week or two later, the ladybird then emerges from the pupa

with unspotted yellow wing cases. The fully-grown adult male and female ladybirds both have spots and look similar.

7. (A) The ladybirds mate and the life cycle of the ladybird then repeats itself.

(B) Ladybirds mate. Life cycle of the ladybird repeats itself.

A. Eggs darken

B. Pupa

C The new-born larva

D. Larva hatching

E. Fully-grown larva

F. Adult ladybird

G. Emerging from the pupa

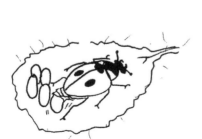

H. Larva eating an aphid

I. Laying eggs

J. Mating

Section 2

Writing Practice for Task 2

CONTENTS

Exercise 1: the functions of sentences

When you reach a certain stage in writing you need to learn not just about words, but about what sentences mean and how they are connected. Of course, people who write fluently are not conscious of this. However, if you want to learn to be a competent writer, you need to know how information and ideas fit together. Greater awareness of the meaning of sentences may at first slow you down. This is a natural process, which occurs in learning any skill. Gradually, however, your fluency, flexibility and competence in writing will increase.

In this exercise, you are going to look at the meaning of individual sentences. Read the sentences below, each of which contains one idea, and choose the function of each sentence from the alternatives given. Note that in some cases there may be more than one correct answer.

If you find the exercise difficult, check your answers with the Key and try the exercise again later.

The functions of three examples have been marked for you in italics.

- Water boils at 100%.
  (a) *a fact* (b) an opinion (c) a proposal (d) a reservation
- The pace of growth will slow down.
  (a) *a prediction* (b) a fact (c) an opinion (d) a suggestion
- Admission charges for school children could be abolished.
  (a) a fact *(b) an example (c) a tentative proposal* (d) a reservation

Now choose the appropriate function(s) for each of the sentences below.

1. Copper is a good conductor of electricity.
   (a) a fact (b) an opinion (c) a proposal (d) a reservation
2. The new motorway may be built in the near future.
   (a) a fact (b) a possibility (c) permission (d) a solution
3. The new motorway can be built in the near future.
   (a) a fact (b) a possibility (c) permission (d) a solution
4. A new bypass around the town should be built underground.
   (a) a fact (b) a possibility (c) permission (d) a suggestion
5. In the UK, the population growth is set to remain flat.
   (a) an opinion (b) a possibility (c) a prediction (d) a result
6. Population growth is increasing in most countries.
   (a) a reservation (b) a measure (c) a fact (d) a general statement
7. The measure cannot be implemented.
   (a) an opinion (b) an impossibility (c) a measure (d) a result
8. The climate changes in the future should make politicians sit up and take notice.
   (a) a fact (b) a possibility (c) an expectation (d) a measure
9. There oughtn't to be any problems after this.
   (a) a fact (b) a possibility (c) a probability (d) a measure
10. The use of mobile phones while driving should have been banned a long time ago.
    (a) a measure (b) a non-fulfilment (c) an improbability (d) a recommendation
11. Local neighbourhoods could be allowed to employ their own security guards to patrol the streets.
    (a) a fact (b) a possibility (c) a probability (d) an example
12. If only the government had acted sooner.
    (a) a measure (b) a regret (c) a probability (d) a proposal

13. They might have increased the chances of winning the prize!
    (a) a fact (b) a possibility (c) a probability (d) a criticism
14. As a result, the programme will not work.
    (a) a result (b) a tentative result (c) a recommendation (d) a conclusion
15. On the spot fines for hooligans are totally unacceptable.
    (a) an opinion (b) a result (c) a tentative result (d) a measure
16. On the spot fines for hooligans are totally unacceptable to many people.
    (a) an opinion (b) a result (c) a general statement (d) a suggestion
17. Crime rates are increasing around the world.
    (a) a conclusion (b) a result (c) a general statement (d) an opinion
18. The measure shouldn't be implemented.
    (a) an opinion (b) a result (c) a negative suggestion (d) a reservation
19. In rich countries, not providing adequate accommodation for all members of society is a criminal act.
    (a) an opinion (b) a result (c) a general statement (d) a conclusion

Exercise 2: functions in more complex sentences

The range of meaning in sentences is very wide, but the way in which you need to combine sentences as you answer Task 2 in the IELTS exam is fairly limited. Look at your own essays, and your friends'. How wide is the range of functions you use? Do you express each function in the same way each time? You will see that the information and the ideas are combined with a limited range of functions.

The sentences below combine two ideas in one sentence. Decide what meaning the part of the sentence *in italics* expresses and choose the appropriate function, or functions, from the alternatives (a-d). Note that there may be more than one answer in each case. When you have finished this exercise, compare the sentences and the functions with the previous exercise.

Example

Universities could be improved by a number of measures like investing money in computers and paying higher salaries to retain experienced staff.
(a) a fact (b) a reservation (c) a probability (d) *a tentative suggestion*

The idea *in italics* is expressed as a tentative suggestion; it is not a strong suggestion, which is why the writer uses *could*.

Now do the same with the sentences below.

1. If more and more money is spent on bureaucracy and administration, *there is less available for other more important causes*.
   (a) a condition (b) an example (c) a result (d) a tentative suggestion
2. The rate of exchange should then decline, *giving companies a welcome breathing space*.
   (a) a result (b) an explanation (c) a probability (d) a fact
3. In secondary school, young people can be encouraged to contribute to the community *by doing voluntary work for old people or by cleaning up the environment*.
   (a) examples (b) an explanation (c) a proposal (d) an effect
4. Because the experience of the elderly is in danger of being lost, *institutions should be forced to employ more and more people over the age of 60*.
   (a) a reason (b) a proposal (c) a result (d) a possibility

5. *Although I agree with the idea*, I have some reservations.
   (a) a suggestion (b) a probability (c) a concession (d) a contrast
6. *Because more and more money is being spent on bureaucracy and administration*, there is less available for other more important causes.
   (a) an example (b) a reason (c) a result (d) an effect
7. *More attention could be focused on literacy and numeracy at secondary level*, as this would raise the employability of youngsters when they leave school.
   (a) an example (b) a method (c) a tentative proposal (d) an effect
8. *If procedures are not tightened up*, the system will break down.
   (a) a result (b) an example (c) a purpose (d) a condition
9. *Being aware of the dangers of smoking more than ever before*, people should generally smoke less.
   (a) a reason (b) a suggestion (c) a result (d) an effect
10. The incidence of drug-related crime has risen rather dramatically in recent years, *but there is a raft of measures being brought in by the present government to tackle the situation*.
    (a) a contrast (b) a suggestion (c) a concession (d) a general situation
11. *Knowing the extent of the problem*, the government needs to take action soon.
    (a) a reason (b) an obligation (c) a proposal (d) a measure
12. Despite the criticism levelled at the government, *not much more could have been done*.
    (a) a conclusion (b) a measure (c) a fact (d) a general situation
13. *This may seem, at first sight, to be a good idea*, but, if one digs just below the surface, the problems soon start to appear.
    (a) a concession (b) a measure (c) a fact (d) a recommendation

Exercise 3: more function pairs

This exercise is a development of Exercise 2. Each text below contains two ideas, which are expressed by two functions. Some of the ideas are combined in one sentence and others are in two sentences linked together. Decide what the function of each part of the text is. For each text put the functions in order.

When you have finished this exercise compare the sentences and the functions with the previous exercise.

Note that each part of a sentence may have more than one function.

1. More nursery school places ought to be provided, because more mothers will then be able to go to work.
   (a) a proposal (b) a recommendation (c) a reservation (d) a reason (e) a result
2. So that more mothers will be able to go to work, more nursery school places ought to be provided.
   (a) a proposal (b) a recommendation (c) a purpose (d) a reason (e) a result
3. The cost of certain drugs should be free: they are much too expensive for poor countries to afford.
   (a) an opinion (b) a measure (c) an explanation (d) a reason (e) a result
4. A good idea would be to make citizen classes compulsory in all schools, which might reduce the incidence of unsociable behaviour.
   (a) a suggestion (b) a strong result (c) a tentative result (d) an effect (e) a reservation
5. A good idea would be to make citizen classes compulsory in all schools, thus reducing the incidence of unsociable behaviour.
   (a) a suggestion (b) a result (c) a tentative result (d) an effect (e) a reservation

6. A good idea would be to make citizen classes compulsory in all schools so that the incidence of unsociable behaviour is reduced.
    (a) a suggestion (b) a result (c) a purpose (d) an example (e) a solution
7. The situation needs to be tackled now; otherwise, the whole network will collapse.
    (a) a suggestion (b) an obligation (c) a result (d) a purpose (e) a probability
8. Consumer confidence must have increased. Otherwise, there wouldn't be so many people spending money in the sales.
    (a) a suggestion (b) a conclusion (c) an effect (d) an example (e) a cause
9. Although the number of young people accessing computer-oriented courses is increasing, yet there is still a serious shortage of skilled people.
    (a) a contrast (b) a concession (c) a result (d) a conclusion (e) a probability
10. Having more training on how to conduct themselves at interviews, the jobless will fare better in the job market.
    (a) a contrast (b) an effect (c) a result (d) a reason (e) a cause
11. Not enough money has been put into the infrastructure. Consequently, it is deteriorating rapidly.
    (a) a contrast (b) an effect (c) a result (d) a reason (e) a cause
12. Aware that the situation might lead to civil disobedience on a large scale, the government ought to have been careful.
    (a) a reason (b) a cause (c) an expectation (d) an effect
13. There will be considerable opposition to this idea. Nevertheless, it needs to be considered fully.
    (a) a concession (b) an effect (c) a contrast (d) a reason (e) a reservation
14. The numbers of people on anti-depressants are increasing dramatically: in the last year alone, figures have almost doubled in certain areas.
    (a) an explanation (b) a general statement (c) a result (d) a reason (e) a cause
15. The repercussions here are extremely serious. For example, there is a strong possibility that we will be facing all out war.
    (a) a reservation (b) a general statement (c) a criticism (d) an example

Exercise 4: common or logical combinations

When you write, do you notice that certain sentences and clauses 'stick together'? There are some types of sentences which combine very frequently with others. You can see in the example in the exercise below that the word *if* indicates that the rest of the sentence is probably going to give a result. When we are writing, we are constantly predicting what the next part of our text will be.

Example:

1/18 or 18/1.

Write the numbers in order: *1/18 or 18/1*. Some combinations may only occur in one order.

Note all the punctuation and capital letters for the beginning of sentences have been removed. Note you may use each text once only.

Now look at the rest of the texts 1-22 below and decide which two texts you can combine.

1. *if more money is invested in management training*

2. another possibility would be to make practical subjects like woodwork compulsory in all schools

3. the government needs to take action against football hooliganism soon

4. the cost of housing for essential workers living in city centres ought to be subsidised

5. otherwise it will deteriorate rapidly

6. but it must not be confused with change for change's sake

7. being more aware of the benefits of a healthy diet than ever before

8. the number of people joining teaching unions has increased

9. many workers will lose their jobs

10. so that they are preserved for future generations

11. because it is now much too expensive for certain key workers to afford

12. nothing whatsoever is being done

13. knowing the extent of the problem

14. thus decreasing the over-emphasis on academic subjects

15. areas of the world like Antarctica should be left untouched

16. in fact membership has gone up quite impressively

17. unless productivity is increased

18. *industrial output will increase dramatically*

19. we should all be avoiding junk food

20. although the situation is desperate

21. the situation needs to be tackled now

22. it is obvious that innovation needs to be encouraged

Exercise 5: flexibility in combining sentences

Most students of writing can tell you many connecting words, but they are limited in their use of these words, or they use the same words again and again without realising it. However, when writing you need to be as flexible as possible.

Insert the appropriate connecting words and phrases from the list below into the pairs of sentences, which follow. Keep the meaning of the sentences in each pair the same. You may use some of the items from the list more than once and in some cases there may be more than one answer.

Connector list

i.	otherwise	x.	although …yet …	xix.	in order to
ii.	much as	xi.	however	xx.	so as not
iii.	so	xii.	so much so	xxi.	nevertheless
iv.	once	xiii.	moreover	xxii.	while
v.	so … that …	xiv.	even so	xxiii.	despite
vi.	although	xv.	so that	xxiv.	Take ….This …
vii.	therefore	xvi.	but	xxv.	For example
viii.	having	xvii.	as well as		
ix.	as	xviii.	though		

Example:

The answer for 1A is *Moreover*. The second sentence gives additional information. For 1B, the answer is *as well as*. Note the verb in the -ing form after the preposition.

1. A) Personal computers are becoming cheaper and cheaper every year. _____, the functions they are now able to perform make them even more attractive.
   B) _____ becoming cheaper and cheaper every year, the functions of personal computer are now able to perform make them even more attractive.
2. A) _____ what is being suggested is difficult to believe, the idea needs to be considered seriously.
   B) What is being suggested is difficult to believe, _____ the idea needs to be considered seriously.
3. A) _____ it is hard to agree to such sweeping changes, _____ they must be implemented.
   B) It is hard to agree to such sweeping changes. _____, they must be implemented.
4. A) The policy was adopted _____ fraud would be decreased rather than increased.
   B) The policy was adopted _____ decrease rather than increase fraud.
5. A) _____ the President disapproved of the Prime Minister, he still had to accept his nomination.
   B) _____ his disapproval of the Prime Minister, the President still had to accept his nomination.

6. A) Newspapers and magazines need to be made from more recycled paper than the present average of 60%; _____, more and more forests might be endangered.

   B) Newspapers and magazines need to be made from more recycled paper than the present average of 60% _____ to endanger more and more forests.

7. A) There was a sharp decline in the popularity of the party. _____, that happened some considerable time before the present party executives were in place.

   B) There was a sharp decline in the popularity of the party, _____ that happened some considerable time before the present party executives were in place.

8. A) Unpalatable _____ they may be, the changes are necessary.

   B) _____ the changes may be unpalatable, they are necessary.

9. A) The rate of increase in prices has slowed down considerably. _____ that some governments are worried more about deflation then inflation.

   B) The rate of increase in prices has slowed down _____ considerably _____ some governments are worried more about deflation then inflation.

10. A) _____ built up a large network of contacts, the company found it easier to market its products.

    B) _____ they had built up a large network of contacts, the company found it easier to market its products.

11. A) The road toll system proved very successful. _____, the government has decided to back the scheme financially.

    B) The road toll system proved very successful, _____ the government has decided to back the scheme financially.

12. A) _____, introducing stiffer penalties for traffic violations is by far the best way to deal with the increase in road fatalities.

    B) _____ the introduction of stiffer penalties for traffic violations. _____ is by far the best way to deal with the increase in road fatalities.

Exercise 6: directed connections within sentences

Students generally have ideas and information about a topic, but they find it difficult to connect the ideas together. For example, a writer may have the following two pieces of information:

♦ *The rules were introduced.*
♦ *The rules decreased traffic congestion immediately.*

It is possible to join these in the following ways:

♦ *The rules were introduced and they decreased traffic congestion immediately.*
♦ *The rules were introduced and, as a result, they decreased traffic congestion immediately.*
♦ *The rules were introduced. As a result, they decreased traffic congestion immediately.*

Linking information within sentences rather than across sentences is usually quite different. A frequent way of linking the ideas above is using the verb + ing for the second verb:

♦ *The rules were introduced, decreasing traffic congestion immediately.*

The latter part of the sentence is possible, because the two verbs in the original two sentences are in the same tense and have the same subject. Other ways that are common for connecting information and ideas are:

- *the use of with + noun instead of a verb*
- *the use of with + verb + ing*
- *the use of by + noun*
- *the use of by + verb + ing*

- *turning verbs into nouns and using the infinitive.*
- *the use of relatives*
- *the use of while/since plus verb + ing*

Now look at the exercise below and combine the information in each case into one sentence. If you cannot do a particular sentence, leave it and go on to the next. Then check the Key. The important thing is that you learn to combine the information this way. Repeat the exercise several times and think about the mechanism rather than just learning the sentences by heart.

Two sentences have been done as examples:

> *The rules were introduced. The rules increased congestion immediately. (Use verb + ing)*
> The rules were introduced, increasing congestion immediately.
> *Businessmen and lobbyists constantly deny charges of corruption. Businessmen and lobbyists secretly bribe the government. (Use while + verb + ing)*
> *Businessmen and lobbyists constantly deny charges of corruption, while secretly bribing the government.*

1. The government plans to help poorer countries. It plans to cancel all third world debt. (Remove the repetition and use *by*)
2. The rules were introduced. The rules increased congestion immediately. (Put the word *Immediately* at the beginning of the sentence)
3. Government officials have constantly been denying charges of corruption. The government officials have secretly been accepting bribes from businessmen and lobbyists alike. (Use *while*)
4. The government has plans to boost renewable energy generation. The plans will be announced today. The plans will be announced by Geoff Healey. This is his first policy move since he became environment minister. (Remove the repetition in the first three sentences; then use *in* and then *since* + verb + ing)
5. The destruction of historic buildings for whatever reasons is repellent to many people. It is a crime against humanity. (Use verb + ing)
6. Charges for entering city centres will be introduced shortly. The charges will raise the cost of motoring. (Use verb + ing)
7. The local authority is knocking down old tower blocks. The local authority wants to improve the area. (Remove the repetition and use *by*)
8. The project is opposed by both big companies and government departments. The project aims to regenerate all slum areas in the next decade. (Use a relative clause without *which/that* or an auxiliary verb)
9. The decision marks the beginning of real competition in the electricity market. The electricity market was a monopoly for more than a hundred years. New rules took effect in January. The rules will allow ElectCom to license competition. (Use *which/until/*verb + ing)
10. All car companies are now expected to face stiff competition. This follows a damning report from the EU Competition Commission. (Use verb + ing)
11. The fares have risen substantially over recent years, The fares put people off public transport. (Remove the repetition and use verb + ing).
12. Companies need to play on their strengths. Companies need to put more effort into successful areas. Companies need to reduce investment in failing ventures.
    (Remove the repetition, use verb + ing and *while* + verb + ing).
13. The government could force through the construction of cheap houses for essential workers.
    It could purchase all the brown-field sites in major cities. (Use *by* + verb + ing or *by* + noun)

Exercise 7: connections undirected

This exercise gives you further practice in connecting ideas and information. This time, however, there are no guidelines about how you should connect the text. Note that there may be more than one way to link the sentences and you may also be able to think of other ways, which are not in the Key.

1. Mr Forest is president of the company. The president has upset the vice president and the directors. He has proposed to sell the firm to one of their rivals in the field. The sale will allow the president to keep his job, but will remove the other directors.
2. The drop-in centre offers counselling. The drop-in centre is supported by the local church. The drop-in centre is a testament to the government's weakness. The church is outdoing it in providing contraception.
3. Mrs Dunn is chairperson of the committee. The chairperson has alarmed other members. She has bid to change the constitution of the committee. The change will allow the chair more powers.
4. The government plans to extend a proposed renewable energy scheme. It will include development of all new hydro projects. This plan may upset environmentalists. The environmentalists claim that larger projects damage eco-systems and threaten wildlife.
5. The government is expected to face stiff opposition to its proposal. It proposes to ban smoking in all public places. This is for the first time and from the autumn. It follows a report by health experts. The report damns present government policy.
6. The licences to provide the rail service will last 10 years. The licences are intended to help rail companies to secure financial backing. The rail companies will improve punctuality and the standard of service.
7. The government has refused to accept responsibility. The government is trying to smooth things out behind the scenes.
8. Charges for entering all museums and art galleries will soon be dropped. This will hopefully lead to an increase in visitor numbers.
9. The report stated that hospitals should tighten up their appointment procedures. This is a proposal that is strongly supported by patients and medics.
10. Some people think that pollution will be reduced. They think recycling materials like bottles and paper will help.
11. The government had plans to boost voting in elections. The plans were announced last week. The plans were announced by the Home Office Minister. He made the announcement immediately after he took up office.

Exercise 8: transformation for flexibility 1

This exercise and the next one show you how flexible you can be in your writing in the IELTS exam. Use the words after each sentence below to change the way the information in the sentences is combined, while keeping the meaning of the original sentence. Note you should make as few changes as possible.

Example:

The system will deteriorate rapidly and so people will be further delayed.
_____ thus delaying _____.
Answer: *The system will deteriorate rapidly thus delaying people further.*

Note that some changes have been made, but that the meaning is the same. Now change the sentences below and then check your answer with the Key.

1. The underlying cause needs to be addressed rather than tackling the result.
    Instead _____.

2. The proposal to legalise cannabis was rushed through and consequently the number of social problems increased.
    _____, resulting in _____.

3. The venture was not thought through carefully enough and so it failed.
    Not having _____.

4. The system will fall apart soon, because more people are using it.
    With _____.

5. If the government does not recruit more police officers to patrol the streets, the crime rate will increase
    _____; otherwise, _____.

6. I have a number of objections to the introduction of higher taxes on petrol, but, on balance, I support the policy.
    Despite _____.

7. In spite of having some objections to the introduction of higher taxes on petrol, on balance, I support the policy.
    Much _____.

8. The law has been relaxed, and so we can focus resources on more serious matters.
    _____ having _____.

9. This is an idea, which has a number of bad points and a number of good points.
    _____ with _____.

10. The idea may cause some inconvenience to the public, but it will be implemented.
    _____ causing _____.

Exercise 9: transformation for flexibility 2

This exercise is a variation of Exercise 8. There are 10 pairs of sentences below. Keeping the same meaning, add words to the second sentence in each case to complete the connection.

Example:

 ♦ The system will deteriorate rapidly thus delaying people further.
 ♦ The system will deteriorate rapidly, _____ people will be further delayed.
  Answer: so/and so

Now complete the sentences below and then check your answer with the Key.

1. This move has angered environmentalists by destroying rather than preserving the pristine woodland.
    This move has angered environmentalists, _____ it has destroyed rather than preserved the pristine woodland.

2. The government, who were initially planning to build a series of new hospitals, finally pulled out of the venture.
    _____ initially to build a series of new hospitals, the government finally pulled out of the venture.

3. The man took the money and ran away.
    _____ the money, the man ran away.

4. The government made sure that the opposition was crushed and then introduced the bill.
    _____ sure that the opposition was crushed, the government then introduced the bill.

5. The proposals may be unacceptable to a large section of the community, but they still need to be adopted.
    Unacceptable _____ the proposals may be to a large section of the community, they still need to be adopted.

6. Although the proposals are coming in for some heavy criticism, they must be supported.
    _____ coming in for some heavy criticism, the proposals must be supported.

7. Should this measure be adopted, it will have serious repercussions on the world economy.
    _____ this measure is adopted, it will have serious repercussions on the world economy.

8. The manoeuvre should be disguised so that it will not upset anyone.
    The manoeuvre should be disguised _____ to upset anyone.

9. If boxing is not banned or strictly controlled, more fighters will be seriously injured or killed.
    Boxing needs to be banned or strictly controlled; _____, more fighters will be seriously injured or killed.

10. As soon as the fuss about animal-to-human transplants has passed over, there will be another dilemma for people to get worked up about.
    _____ the fuss about animal-to-human transplants has passed over, there will be another dilemma for people to get worked up about.

Exercise 10: simple and effective connections in a paragraph 1

Students often have the main points of what they want to write in their heads. However, they frequently find it difficult to combine the individual pieces of information to form a complex paragraph.

Look at the sentences in the left-hand column below. You can see that each sentence contains a main point. Use the connecting words in the column on the right in the order they occur to create a paragraph. Remove all unnecessary repetition. You will have to change the punctuation and remove some words. For example, you need to remove the words **in bold** in number 2 to in order to use the word *like*. You also need to remove the full stop after *country* at the end of the first sentence.

Sentences	**Connecting words**
1. Money needs to be invested in the infrastructure of the country.	**Unless**
2. **An example is** the transport system.	**like**
3. A number of problems will arise.	
4. The transport system will wear out.	**For example,**
5. The transport system will break down.	**and**
6. The breaking down of the transport system will cause serious inconvenience to the travelling public.	**verb + ing**
7. The break down in the transport system and inconvenience to the travelling public will have a knock-on effect.	**This**
8. It will have a knock-on effect on the economy in general.	**[Remove repetition]**
9. More people will turn to cars.	with + verb + ing
10. The roads will become congested.	and + verb + ing
11. The congested roads will slow the economy down.	which, in turn,

Exercise 11: simple and effective connections in a paragraph 2

This exercise gives you more practice with putting ideas into a text. This time, however, there are no hints as to how you should connect the text. The final paragraph is very similar to the Key to the previous exercise.

You can study the previous exercise and the Key, but when you do the exercise try not to look at either. You could try to do the exercise in your head, before you write it out. Remember that writing is as much, if not more, a mental as it is a physical exercise.

Sentences

1. More public funds in many rich western countries need to be invested in skills shortages in certain areas.

2. An example is teacher training and teaching.

3. There will be serious repercussions.

4. The educational system will deteriorate further.

5. The education system will simply collapse.

6. The collapse of the education system will seriously affect the whole of society.

7. The collapse of the education system will have serious consequences.

8. The collapse of the education system will have serious consequences for companies.

9. The companies will turn to other countries where there are no skills shortages to set up new ventures.

10. In my home country, factories are being built in areas where there is a surplus of skilled computing staff.

11. Governments in more developed countries will have less money from taxes to fund training.

Exercise 12: functions in a text

This exercise gives you more practice with fitting information together. Look at the following text:

Sport has a wide range of benefits. It encourages people from different cultures to come into contact with each other. It helps to break down barriers between different countries. Sport furthers international cooperation.

The text above is correct grammatically and there is some connection. However, the writer does not show how the sentences relate to each other. Below is a passage with 14 sections. In the column on the right, there is a list of functions (A-J), which describe the text. Match the functions to the texts marked 1-14. Note that you can use a function more than once. The first one has been done **in bold** as an example.

Text

1. **Sport has a wide range of benefits.** 2. First, at an international level, it encourages people from different cultures to come into contact with each other, 3. which then helps to break down barriers between different countries. 4. and furthers international cooperation. 5. Take amateur sports meetings between schools and universities in different parts of the world. 6. Many countries arrange contacts of this kind 7. so that people at different levels in their respective societies develop closer bonds, 8. just as happens with cultural exchanges or trade links. 9. This is obviously of mutual benefit to all concerned.

10. While some people are reluctant to take up any kind of activity that involves exertion, 11. playing sport can have a very positive effect on health. 12. All physical exercise improves coordination and, at the same time, increases well-being. 13. In fact, it helps fight against disease, 14. thereby enhancing the quality of people's lives.

Functions

A. a possibility and an advantage

B. a conclusion

C. a result

D. an example

E. an advantage

F. a purpose

G. an explanation

H. a reservation

I. a comparison

J **a focus sentence**

Exercise 13: text jigsaw

The jumbled text below gives you practice with predicting the grammar and the function of a paragraph as you write. Write out the 14 pieces of jumbled text in the correct order.

Remember to use grammar as well as meaning to help you.

The first piece of text has been marked for you **in bold**.

1. *of a nation depends on natural resources, but*

2. *economic, but also the social development of a country suffers.*

3. *nations fail to invest sufficient funds, for one reason or another,*

4. *Unfortunately, many*

5. *skilled and healthy workforce.*

6. *in their health systems.*

7. *For example, the manufacturing industry needs healthy workers*

8. *as do the financial and services sectors. Otherwise, not only the*

9. *A lack of investment in health care, however,*

10. *health plays an equally important role. Every*

11. **It is often said that the wealth**

12. *country requires a*

13. *now suffer from a workforce that cannot function efficiently.*

14. *means that these countries*

Exercise 14: writing by question

This exercise looks at the organisation of writing a paragraph in a different way: by asking yourself questions. Look at your own essays. Do the sentences in each paragraph you write follow a logical series of questions?

On the left, there is a series of questions. Answer these questions from the alternatives in the right-hand column to create a text on poverty and crime.

Questions

Answers

1. **What is poverty like in today's world?**

A Poverty appears to be increasing rather than decreasing even though people generally are becoming richer.
B Poverty is the state where people earn less than the average income.
C Poverty will always be with us.
D The most important cause is poverty.

2. **What do many people think poverty causes?**

A Many people feel that poverty will be wiped out in the future.
B Some people are of the opinion that poverty and crime are closely related.
C Many people think crime is related to poverty.
D Many people believe poverty is the main cause of crime.

3. **But what do I believe?**

A but I think it is a big mistake.
B but they are entitled to their own opinions.
C but I believe that they might be right.
D but I believe that they are seriously mistaken.

4. **What is the first reason for their misconception?**

A For a start, there are more poor people than rich people.
B More poor people than rich people appear to be caught committing serious crimes.
C This misconception arises simply because poverty is getting worse.
D Poor people annoy rich people.

5. **And the result?**

A It is not true, because it takes time.
B It is not true, because poverty is with us always.
C So statistically there is a good chance of there being more crimes which are committed by poor people.
D Poor people have just the same rights as the rich.

6. **What other reason can I add?**

A There are always other reasons.
B Further, there are many criminals around who come from the rich or upper-classes, but they can employ people to help them avoid being caught.
C Further, poverty will always be with us.
D And I can think of many other reasons.

7. **What is my conclusion?**

A So, the fact that poverty is the main cause of crime is not a fallacy.
B So, the fact that poverty is the main cause of crime is a fallacy.
C If only the government had more money to tackle the problem.
D The government will introduce a raft of new measures to tackle the problem.

When you have checked your answer with the Key. Think about the questions in the left-hand column and try to write your own paragraph. You can do this by using the text in the right-hand column as your guide. You can also do it without looking at the text.

Before you write your next essay, you may want to read the questions in this exercise to help create some guidelines.

Exercise 15: more questions for guided writing

In this exercise you are going to create a paragraph from jumbled sentences with the help of questions. Look at the two columns below. On the left, there is a series of questions. On the right, you can see that some of the questions have been answered, but most are blank. Use the list of answers (a – j) below to complete the text. There are more answers than questions, so you will not use all of them.

Questions

What is education?

What do some people think about it?

What do other people think about it?

What do I think? Do I agree with them?

What is the main effect of education?

How does it give an individual freedom?

Can I be more specific/give a more specific example?

And another specific example?

What is the opposite, i.e. the effect of no education?

Can I give a specific example?

What is then the general effect of the lack of IT skills?

Answers

_____1_____.

Some people think that it is a basic right like food and water,

_____2_____.

Personally, I believe that education should be totally free.

_____3_____

_____4_____.

_____5_____.

Further, they can improve themselves as individuals.

_____6_____.

_____7_____.

_____8_____.

List of answers

a) by giving people a tool with which they can improve their lives.

b) As a consequence, the progress of entire countries, not just individuals, is being held up.

c) Education is not free for everyone in the world.

d) Conversely, a lack of education limits all members within a society.

e) First of all, education gives an individual freedom

f) The current shortage of IT skills, even in developed countries, is a good example.

g) Education is a basic necessity in the modern world.

h) while others believe that some payment should be made for education.

i) Individuals can, for instance, improve their job prospects if they gain qualifications.

j) As a consequence, the progress of entire countries, not just individuals, will benefit.

Exercise 16: text from a semi-jigsaw

In the exercise below, the sentence beginnings in the column on the left are in the correct order. To complete the sentences and create a paragraph, match the jumbled sentence ends in the column on the right.

You can use each text on the right only once. The first complete sentence has been done for you in bold.

1. **Planting more trees in city centres ...**

2. The trees, as well as ...

3. There ...

4. Any green space,

5. The city of London, where there are many parks, ...

6. In many other cities, lines of trees ...

7. Moreover, the leaves ...

8. Along with trees, fountains in public places ...

9. The sound of falling or flowing water ...

10. Many people, for instance, enjoy ...

a) can also help to make the environment in cities more appealing.

b) watching water as a form of escape from the stresses of work.

c) is a very good example.

d) making the environment more pleasant to live and work in, will add a touch of colour.

e) is very restful.

f) however small, provides welcome relief from the endless concrete.

g) **is yet another way to make the surroundings attractive.**

h) are planted on streets to provide shade in the summer for pedestrians and workers.

i) contribute to making the air fresher.

j) is certainly nothing more attractive than greenery in parks or gardens or on drab city streets.

Exercise 17: four-way jumble

The jigsaw in this exercise is slightly more complex than in the previous exercise. You can see that there are three columns. Choose an item from each column to make seven sentences, which, you then put in order to form a paragraph on solving congestion in city centres. You may use each item only once.

The paragraph contains the following 7 functions:

a solution, a result, a reaction, an explanation, a result, a [second] result and a conclusion.

Use these functions to help you put the sentences in order. The first sentence, *a solution,* has been marked for you *in italics.*

A	B	C
1. A further deterrent is that the restriction to people's movements	a) is	i. necessary.
		ii. *charging for private cars entering city centre areas.*
	b) is paying	
2. What people will object to most	c) *is to introduce*	iii. going into the central zone.
3. Without doubt, the restrictions	d) are	iv. extra revenue which which can be spent on public transport.
4. Yet, conscious of the cost, car owners	e) will be discouraged from	v. not difficult to imagine.
5. *The best solution*		vi. the extra money.
6. The initial public reaction. however,	f) will raise	vii. their attitudes and the congestion in city centres.
7. Such charges	g) will affect	

Exercise 18: speed ordering

By now you should be much faster at putting texts together. In the exercise below, the texts between sentences 1 and 6 are jumbled and one of them is irrelevant. The texts between 6 and 14 are also jumbled, but four are irrelevant.

As quickly as you can, put the sentences into the correct order to create a paragraph

When you have checked your answer with the Key, try to write your own text on the same subject using sentences 1, 6 and 14 as a guide.

1. **Many people are pressing for more and more recycling.**

2. However, it has been shown that more energy is used when items are recycled.

3. They say that valuable resources are being wasted by throwing away newspapers, food packaging batteries and bottles, etc.

4. Newspapers provide us with up-to-date information.

5. Already some newspapers are made from more than 60% recycled paper and the amount is increasing.

6. **People forget about the petrol required to transport the waste in large lorries and the exhaust fumes from the vehicles.**

7. Research provides helpful information.

8. Energy is as everyone knows a very valuable resource.

9. Some of the packaging, which is used is very attractive.

10. Research should also be carried out to find other less harmful ways of recycling bottles and other waste.

11. Similarly, the recycling process requires energy as well! Instead of recycling waste, the amount of packaging in wrapping food should be reduced.

12. In the future, there will be e-newspapers and e-books so the anxiety of disposing of waste paper will be reduced.

13. So the amount of non-recycled paper is 48%.

14. **But then we will have something else to be anxious about!**

Exercise 19: mixed connections

This exercise gives practice with increasing your flexibility and fluency in connecting your ideas. Choose suitable connections from the alternatives A, B, C, D in the texts below.

Note that in some instances, there may be more than one suitable answer.

1. There has been a sharp increase in the different types of mobile phones coming on to the market. (A. *The sharp increase in the different types* B. *This, however,* C. *A sharp increase in the different types* D. *However, it.*) is happening at a time when the market place is saturated.

2. The government has ambitious plans to connect every home to the Internet. (A. *Doing that* B. *Were the government to do this, it* C. *They* D. *To do so*) would require considerable resources.

3. It is difficult to choose between the two arguments. (A. *Both issues are* B. *They are both* C. *Both are* D. *Both the arguments that are difficult are*) equally valid.

4. The research found serious faults with a number of operational procedures, but little attention was paid to (A. *it* B. *the findings* C. *the research* D. *the research about serious faults*).

5. The rate of increase in prices has slowed down considerably. (A. *So much so* B. *The rate has slowed down so much* C. *It has slowed down so much* D. *So much*) that some governments are worried more about deflation than inflation.

6. The finance minister resigned suddenly this week. (A. *It* B. *A minister's resignation* C. *Resignation* D. *This sensational event*) will certainly have an unsettling effect on the markets.

7. Most people would never have believed (A. *this* B. *it* C. *that* D. *what is to follow*): the government has decided to back the scheme financially.

8. Sales rose in a rather desultory manner for the first few months, but (A. *a rise* B. *the increase* C. *the rise* D. *it*) was short-lived as shares slumped.

9. The off-shore oil exploration programme failed, because the financial backers withdrew their support from (A. *it* B. *the venture* C. *this* D. *the off-shore oil exploration programme*).

10. (A. *They had* B. *They* C. *Having* D. *Once they had*) built up a large network of contacts, the company found it easier to market its products.

Exercise 20: more mixed connections

This exercise gives more practice with connecting your ideas. Choose suitable alternatives in the texts below. Note in some instances there may be more than one suitable answer.

1. Animal welfare is one of today's burning political issues. Nor does it look as if *(A. the issue B. the subject C. this D. it)* will fade from view in the near future.

2. Many people in north European countries choose holidays in Spain. *(A. In Spain B. There C. In that country D. Over there)* the sun shines uninterrupted for days on end.

3. A series of natural disasters followed one another in quick succession. *(A. These B. The event C. These events D. It)* happened faster than the emergency services could cope with.

4. The number of young people staying on in education after the age of 16 has risen sharply in recent years, but *(A. it B. they C. this improvement D. changes)* may not be sustainable.

5. Provided the government increases salaries in the public sector, they will be able to attract staff of the right calibre. Few ministers, however, will be able to accept *(A. such a condition B. a condition C. condition D. it)*.

6. All vehicles except for ambulances and bicycles have been banned from the area. *(A. This B. It C. The ban D. The restriction)* will remain in force for the foreseeable future.

7. Deforestation of the area has taken place at a much quicker pace recently to make way for farms. *(A. They B. Unfortunately, many of the trees C. Unfortunately, they D. Unfortunately, many of them)* are rare and irreplaceable.

8. Anyone who commits a crime, however minor, ought to be imprisoned. *(A. It B. To carry out such a proposal C. To do such D. The recommendation)* would require a considerable sum of money.

9. While many people object to the legalisation of cannabis, *(A. it B. decriminalisation C. this D. idea)* is not as crazy as it first appears.

10. Many elderly people are still living in poverty, *(A. a situation which B. this C. but this D. the situation)* is gradually changing.

Exercise 21: connections for flexibility and fluency

When writing an essay, it is sometimes difficult to avoid repetition and at the same time to write fluently. This requires a high degree of flexibility. In this exercise, you are going to focus on avoiding repeating yourself while connecting a text.

Look at the list of items A-V below. Then read the text, which follows the list, and choose suitable items from the list to connect the text. Note that in some cases more than one answer may be possible.

Remember to avoid repetition.

A. people who make too much noise
B. this
C. it
D. these
E. people making too much noise
F. such anti-social behaviour
G. noisy people
H. loud music from neighbours
I. is another source of annoyance
J. if people living in flats play hi-fi systems etc too loudly, they
K. people living in flats who play hi-fi systems etc too loudly

L. anti-social behaviour of this kind
M. flat-dwellers who play hi-fi systems etc too loudly
N. those making too much noise
O. they
P. also constitutes a source of annoyance
Q. these curbs
R. another thing that is annoying
S. such rudeness in shops or over the telephone
T. such rudeness
U. nuisance
V. such offending drivers

Noise, especially loud music from neighbours in blocks of flats, is a major nuisance. _____1_____ is now such a frequent occurrence that the present law should be made even stricter to curb _____2_____. _____3_____ should be warned once only in writing and then speedily evicted. Loud music from cars passing or parked outside in the street _____4_____. As well as seizing the equipment, be it a car radio or the car itself, _____5_____ should have their licences endorsed. _____6_____ on bad behaviour may not deter the seasoned offender, but _____7_____ will reduce the _____8_____.

_____9_____ is people being rude, for example, shoppers who jump queues or shop assistants who do not know how to deal with customers. The public needs to complain more and more about _____10_____. Seeking compensation from organisations might also help.

Exercise 22: not enough spaces

Look at the list of items below and then the text, which follows. You can see that there are 15 items in the list, but only 10 spaces (A – J). However, all of the items in the list need to be inserted somewhere in the text. Use the punctuation and grammar of the items to help you. Note you may use each item only once.

One item has been inserted for you.

1. or
2. but
3. They point to
4. which
5. Moreover, whilst such farms
6. A further downside is
7. of the opinion
8. **people, however,**

9. The same arguments apply
10. unless perhaps they
11. The obvious objections here
12. being nothing
13. they
14. the machines
15. of bringing the energy back to the shore

Other are _____A_____ that wind farms are ugly, _____B_____ more than an eyesore _____C_____ a blot on the landscape. the fact that the giant wind turbines, make up the farms are frequently built in remote areas of great beauty. _____ D _____ are inaccessible to most people, _____E_____ can be seen from a great distance. _____F_____ that wind farms may provide safer alternatives to nuclear power or carbon based energy, _____G_____ they cause greater damage than the pollution are intended to prevent. _____H_____ to windmills at sea, _____I_____ are far enough off the coast not to be seen. _____J_____ are the cost of siting the wind turbines far out to sea and.

Exercise 23: essay titles

It is important that you are able to interpret essay titles in the exam so that you write an essay that answers the question. Your sentences need to fit together to form a paragraph and the paragraphs need to fit the essay question, not just almost fit.

Look at the pairs of essay titles below. Decide what the similarities and differences are between each essay in the pair. The first one has been done for you.

1.   **A**   *What are the main causes of crime?*
     B   *Crime is a major problem for many societies throughout the world and is increasing rather than decreasing. What are the main reasons for crime?*

There are two basic similarities between the two essays. In each essay, the general subject is crime and the essay is organised around focus words: causes and reasons for, which both mean the same thing. The difference is that the first essay title is presented as a question, whereas the second one makes a statement about the present situation as regards crime and then poses a question. In the end, the content and organisation of the essays are basically the same..

2.   **A**   Only education can tackle anti-social behaviour, such as football hooliganism and vandalism. Measures such as <u>fines</u> and <u>prison sentences</u> or <u>curfews</u> do not work. How far do you agree?
     B   Only measures such as fines and prison sentences or curfews can tackle anti- social behaviour such as football hooliganism and vandalism. Education does not have any effect. To what extent do you agree?
3.   **A**   How far do you agree or disagree that it is only education and not other measures such as fines and prison sentences or curfews that can tackle anti-social behaviour, such as football hooliganism and vandalism?
     B   The only way to combat crime is through education. To what extent do you agree?
4.   **A**   Charging people for plastic bags in supermarkets and refunding money on glass bottles were once the norm in some countries. Do you think that this is the best way to make people more aware of the damage plastic bags and bottles cause to the environment?
     B   Discuss the best ways to make people aware of the need to care for wildlife.
5.   **A**   The abuse of animals, both wild and domestic, is increasing year by year. The numbers of species of wild animal are decreasing through pressure on their habitat from man and cruelty to domestic animals including pets is a serious problem. How can this cruelty be stopped? What benefits do animals bring the human race?
     B   The abuse of animals, both wild and domestic, is increasing year by year. The numbers of species of wild animal are decreasing through pressure on their habitat from man and cruelty to domestic animals including pets is a serious problem. Should there be stiffer penalties for the abuse of animals? What factors are involved in this abuse?
6.   **A**   What factors are involved in making people in the modern world feel insecure?
     B   People in the modern world feel more insecure than they used to be. Discuss the causes of this.
7.   **A**   People in the modern world feel more insecure than they used to be. Do you agree?
     B   People in the modern world feel more insecure than they used to be. How far do you agree or disagree?
8.   **A**   Modern technology like computers and mobile phones is more of a problem for parents than it is for their children. How far do you agree? In what ways can adults be encouraged to embrace new technology?
     B   Violence is one of the major scourges of the modern age. Can anything can be done to tackle this problem? Or is violence just an inevitable consequence of modern life?

9.   **A**   It is important in today's world to have as broad an education as possible. Discuss the arguments for or against this issue.

     B   Success is seen by many as a goal. However, it does have a downside. What are the major disadvantages of being successful?

10. **A**   More and more people throughout the world are using credit cards in one form or another. So much so that the end of the cash age is being predicted. Are we moving towards a totally cash free world? Or do you think that cash is here to stay?

     B   More and more people throughout the world are using credit cards in one form or another. So much so, in fact, that the end of the cash age is being predicted. Discuss the problems that might arise if this, in fact, happened.

Exercise 24: same information- different paragraphs

When candidates are preparing for the exam, they frequently learn essays by heart and then try to fit them into the question they have in the exam. It is possible to have an essay, which has a similar general subject to one you have prepared, but which has a different focus. Unless your English is fluent or very competent, however, it is difficult to fit the paragraphs you have learnt into another essay.

Read through the text below and then look at the four lists of items, which follow. Write out the text and insert the items from each list to create four different paragraphs. The items are in the order which you should use them. Please note that in some cases you will have to makes changes to the text. Look at the Key for the first paragraph to help you if necessary.

> The large number of people living in poor accommodation only stores up problems for the future. Poor housing is a major breeding ground for a vast array of social as well as economic ills. Those living in poor conditions are caught in a cycle of despair. This affects both their physical and mental health. This is a burden on any country's resources. The health and other services have to deal with the situation. Poor housing requires continuous costly repairs to the buildings. This is a further drain on resources.

Paragraph 1: Example: Some believe that the large number of people …

Paragraph 1 - Neutral	**Paragraph 1 - Opinion 1**
a) Some believe that …	a) In my opinion, …
b) They think that …	b) The main reason for this is … which …
c) For example, on the social front, …	c) Take, for example,… who …
d) affecting	d) The consequent effects on …
e) [This …], in turn, …	e) where ….
f) … where …	f) Similarly,
g) Secondly, on the purely economic front, ..	g) further …
h) which …	

Paragraph 3 - Cause and effect

a)   The main cause is … which …
b)   as
c)   First
d)   which
e)   and …also …
f)   …then …
g)   Furthermore, …
h)   – a …

Paragraph 4 - Opinion 2

a)   My main argument is that …
b)   … , to all intents and purposes, …
c)   For example,…
d)   which, as a result, …
e)   They then become ….
f)   … with ….
g)   Another problem is that …
h)   which further…

Exercise 25: maze for flexibility – pre-writing task

You can use this exercise to help you revise the mechanisms you have learnt in this section of the book. Read through the maze below and choose the alternative which you like the best at each step. Please note that all the alternatives are correct. For example, you can choose 1A and then 2C.and so on. Or, you can choose all of column A.

A	B	C
1. Travelling is a good example to illustrate how important non-school education is.	A good example to illustrate the importance of non-school education is travelling.	Travelling is a good example to illustrate the importance of non-school education.
2. A rather sophisticated learning process is taking place for travellers	People go through a rather sophisticated learning process	People are being subjected to a rather subtle education process
3. when they visit new places abroad as tourists.	when visits are made to new places abroad.	when new places abroad are being visited.
4. They are, for instance, learning about the culture of other countries, the geography etc ,	They are learning about the geography etc of other countries,	They are learning about the geography, the culture, the history and language of other countries,
5. thereby hopefully broadening their horizons.	and hopefully broadening their horizons.	and hopefully their horizons are broadened.
6. Moreover,	A further effect is that	Secondly,
7. travelling builds self-confidence,	travelling helps to build self-confidence,	travelling is a great confidence builder,
8. as people learn to deal with different challenges.	by teaching people to cope with different situations.	as it teaches people to handle different problems.
9. Once they have, say, mastered simple procedures like buying a train ticket or changing currency,	When simple procedures like buying a train ticket have been mastered,	Simple procedures like buying a train ticket having been mastered,
10. travellers are then able to tackle more complex situations.	an attempt can be made at tackling even more complex situations.	even more complex situations can be attempted.
11. If, however, people just remain within their own narrow circle, then their experiences are narrow.	By contrast, remaining within their own narrow circle, limits people's experiences and, hence, their expectations.	On the other hand, by just staying put, people's experiences are narrow and their expectations limited.

Try not to learn the texts by heart. Instead, before you write an essay, read through the maze and as you do so, try to transform the text as you read. This will help you become faster as you write and increase your flexibility.

Section 3

Checking and Editing

CONTENTS

Exercise 1: speed spelling check

In the IELTS exam, candidates do not always leave themselves time to check their writing for mistakes such as spelling. This is, however, a habit and a skill you need to develop.

In the list below, there are 50 words. Read through the list as quickly as you can and find words which have the wrong spelling and then correct them.

dramatically motivation peopl experience environment goverment unfortunatly colleague accommodation seperate plummet thier conection conscientous discreet difference difficult advantage dissappear disappointment interested disposess dissolve disuade efficient efficiency embarrassed dictionary unpleasent secretary comfortable counsel programm parliment interesting psychology simultaneously house television institution inconvinience incapable forecast responsable machine manufacture scarse scenery vehical sheild

Exercise 2: spelling check – same words different presentation

Now look at the same list from Exercise 1 again below. Note the words have been jumbled. Read through the list as quickly as you can and this time find the words, which are spelt correctly. Then correct those words, which are spelt wrongly.

responsible manufacture incapible council programme eficient mashine coleague television instution inconvenence scarse scenry motivation people experience enviroment government unfortunately conection conscentious unplesant discrete diffrence dificult advantige dissappear dissapointment drammatically Interested dispossess disolve dissuade efficiency embarassed dictionry secretary comfortible plummet their parliament intresting psichology simultanously house forcast vehicle shield seperate acommodation

Exercise 3: identifying correct spelling - speed checking

Being able to recognise correct spelling as well as mistakes is important; otherwise, you may change something which is already correct. Read through the lists of words below as quickly as you can and *find only words which are spelt correctly*. Then go through the list again and correct the mistakes.

Note there may be more than one correct spelling in each line.

1. tomorrow support should recieve proffesional

2. serious salary review receipt feild recommend

3. pronounciation photograph permanent particular

4.   organise opportunity neighbour necessary morover

5.   misrable judgment interupt interfer height

6.   generous foreign favourite familiar extrordinary

7.   mention excellent esential entertainment encourag

8.   elswhere sieze therefor although thorough

9.   potatoe whether wonderfull yesterday atmospher

10. accurate apparatus chanel chocolate ciggarette

11. circuit correspondance equivalent hereditry irritate

12. February vegitable chimeney shoulder cronology

13. circelation campain succesful stationry surroundings

14. probabilty priceless prevalent postpon pleasure

15. phenomenon plentifull personel persistance percieve

Exercise 4: identifying more correct spelling

By now you should be a little faster. Read through the lists of words below as quickly as you can and find words which are spelt correctly. When you have checked the whole list and located the correct spellings, go through the list again and correct the mistakes.

Note there may be more than one correct spelling in each line.

1.   Circumstance disease disguis gaurantee discriminate

2.   Disperate hypothesis themometer metaphor appropriate

3.   Beleive misellaneous concieve mispelling beginning

4.   Benifit dangrous membrane ceremony droped

5.   Circle citisen clearence trafic co-operate Antartica

6.   Recomendation commitee commitment complementry

7.   Consceince science contrary arguement cultural

8.   Techniqu cynical desiccated democracy demographic

9.   Emergenc excesive prerequisite featur ferocious

10. Flight analisis gallop gratuitous genine great

Exercise 5: spelling completion 1

In this exercise, there are some common words from which the vowels have been removed. However, even with just the consonants, you can see that in many cases you can recognise the word, but can you spell it correctly?

Look at words 1 – 20 and write out the correct spelling on a separate sheet of paper. You may find that it is refreshing to do this exercise again quickly before you write an essay. When you repeat it, it is not necessary to write it out. You can do it in your head.

Add the vowels **a e i o u** or **y** to make words, e.g. c_t . You add the vowel a to make cat.

1.   t_l_v_s_ _n
2.   t_l_ph_n_
3.   b_c_cl_
4.   c_ntr_v_rs_
5.   _nc_ _ r_g_
6.   h_z_rd
7.   _nd_ng_r

8.   p_t_t_
9.   _ndl_ss
10. w_rthl_ss
11. w_nd_rf_l
12. b_ _ _ t_f_l
13. f_m_l_ _r_se
14. f_m_l_

15. _nf_rm_t_ _n
16. g_ _ d_l_n_
17. c_nsc_ _ nt _ _ _ s
18. h_p_f_l
19. _dv_ rt_ s _m _nt
20. _d_ c_t _ _ n

Exercise 6: spelling completion 2

This exercise gives you more practice in completing words by adding the vowels.

Look at words 1 – 25 and write out the correct spelling on a separate sheet of paper. You may find that it is refreshing to do this exercise again quickly before you write an essay. When you repeat it, it is not necessary to write it out. You can do it in your head.

Add the vowels **a e i o u** or **y** to make words, e.g. c_t . You add the vowel a to make cat.

1.   _nc_d_nc_
2.   c_ns_q_ _ntl_
3.   _nv_r_nm_nt
4.   g_v_rnm_nt
5.   _nt_rv_n_
6.   _ntr_d_c_
7.   l_rg_l_
8.   _ll_t_r_t_
9.   m_gn_f_c_nt

10. m_x_m_m
11. m_n_m_m
12. d_cl_n_
13. pl_mm_t
14. tr_nd
15. c_ntr_st
16. pr_d_ct
17. f_r_c_st
18. pl_ng_

19. r_ck_t
20. tr_ _gh
21. _c_ n_m_c
22. c_n _m_
23. p_ rt_c_l_rl_
24. pr_ g r_m m_
25. b_ s _n_ ss

Exercise 7: what is it?

This exercise is designed to be done several times. Do not expect to get all of the answers correct at the first attempt.

Look at the list of 21 incomplete words below. You can see that most of the consonants have been removed and it is now more difficult to recognise the words. Add the consonants: b c d f g h j k l m n p q r s t v w x z to make words:

Example: _e_e_ _o_e [telephone]

If you do not recognise a word, leave it and go on to the next. If you have to, look at the Key and check the answers. Leave the exercise and do it again another time, especially before you write an essay. Note that you may be able to make more than one word in each case.

1.   _ e a
2.   i _ e a
3.   _ a i _
4.   _ a _ a _ a
5.   _ o u _ e
6.   e i _ _ t
7.   _ e i _ _ _
8.   _ _ e i _
9.   _ e _ e i _ e
10. _ e _ i e _ e
11. a _ a i _ a _ _ e

12. _ a _ i o u _
13. _ a _ i e _ y
14. i _ t e _ e _ _
15. e _ o u _ _
16. _ _ i e _ _
17. _ e a _ u _ e
18. _ e e _ i _ g
19. _ e _ e _ i _ i o _
20. _ e _ e _ _ o _ e
21. e _ o _ o _ i c

Exercise 8: more difficult words to complete

This exercise like Exercise 7 is designed to be done several times. Do not expect to get all of the answers correct at the first attempt.

Below is another list of common incomplete words. You can see that many of the consonants have been removed, but there are more consonants than in the previous exercise. Add the consonants: b c d f g h j k l m n p q r s t v w x z to make words:

Example: _ e _ e_ _ o _ e [telephone]

If you do not recognise a word, leave it and go on to the next. If you have to, look at the Key and check the answers. Leave the exercise and do it again another time, especially before you write an essay.

1. e _ _ _ o y e e
2. _ e n t e _ c e
3. _ i _ _ i o n a r y
4. p o _ _ i _ i _ i t y
5. s t _ e _ g t h
6. _ o _ a _ o
7. l i _ _ a r y
8. _ a n _ u a _ e
9. p o _ i _ e _ a n
10. p o _ i _ e _ o _ a _
11. p _ y _ h o _ o _ y

12. e _ _ a u _ t e d
13. e _ _ i r o _ _ e _ t
14. b i _ y _ l e
15. _ a _ g e _ o u s
16. _ o _ _ u t i o n
17. _ o _ f u _ e d
18. _ o n g e _ _ e _
19. _ o l i _ a y
20. _ _ o u _ _ _
21. o u _ _ _
22. d a u _ _ _ e r

23. e x e _ _ i _ e
24. _ o _ i t i _ i a n
25. p e _ m i _ s i o _
26. _ e o _ l e
27. _ e b _ u a r y
28. s e _ _ e _ a r y
29. _ o m _ u _ e r
30. _ o n s _ i o u _

Exercise 9: spelling in sentences

In the sentences below, there are spelling mistakes. Read through the sentences and underline those words that you think may be spelt wrongly. Then check their spelling in a dictionary. There may be more than one spelling mistake in each sentence.

In sentence 1, are the words, which are highlighted spelt correctly?

---

1. The accommodation available to people in lower income groups is usually very inadiquate.

2. A completely new suite of rooms is esential to house the new equipment.

3. Frequently, the planing is not particularly thorough so that when it comes to carrying out any work, there are invarably delays.

4. There are not enouh teachers to provide adequate cover in schools.

5. Invensions in the world of technology are now practicaly a dialy occurence.

6. It is hardly aceptable to expect private buisnesses to shoulder the whole finantial burdon.

7. The remedy applied by most goverments has been to introduce swingeing cuts to thier manpower only to hire them at greater cost, once they realise that they have lost personel with invaluable experience.

8. Guaging the mood of the electorate requires considerable political skill.

9. Everyone has benifited from the advances in the medical feild that we have witnesed in recent years.

10. News buletins are now transmited round the clock, almost overwelming us with up-to-date information.

11. The number of young people entering higher education from poor backgrounds is a shinning example of what can be acheived.

12. Once the idea has been thouht threw carefuly, it will not be long befor everyone is taking it up wholehertedly.

13. Profesionalism in most fields of work is now in such short suply that the best one can hope for is medocrity.

14. Apropriate measures should be taken to insure that rioting does not take place at any sporting event.

15. Some people argue that so many old traditions have been superceded by modern or foriegn ideas that we are in danger of loosing our national identity.

16. Atention should now be focused on equiping as many tertiary level students as possible with laptops.

Exercise 10: jumbled words

In the text below there are 21 words where the letters are jumbled. One of them is marked for you in bold. What is it? Read the text as quickly as you can, find the other 20 jumbled words and write them out.

We cosaesita being rich with not having a care in the **rowld**, with tromcof and feeling safe and secure. thweal is seen as the sanrew to the many problems in life.

Having huge satumon of money at one's diospsal is, ironically, a fudilfict problem to deal with. People are edstepe in the beifle that being rich represents security. But does it? To protect accumulated isosesspons, no matter how small the amount, seemingly countless saemures are needed by the rich, and not so rich, to protect trieh property. The burglar malars and security bars on windows and doors of today, however, will seem pirivmite to the security of the future. The very well-off already living in fortified compounds will have sacecs to hand/iris recognition devices to enter their property. Yet, every solution tends to bring about another scenario to be aedlt with. So, what if the hand is cut off or the eye removed? The answer is make sure the device can only gnisereco live irises and hands. Problem solved. No, not exactly. You can be appedkind. That's where the body-guards come in. But can you trust them? Perhaps, heert is only one way out: if something is scunaig you a problem, the sensible thing to do is to get rid of it!

Exercise 11: missing words

When candidates are writing fast, it is difficult to concentrate on everything at the same time. A common mistake is to leave out words for one reason or another.

The text below is an extract from a much longer passage. There are some places where a word is missing. For example, in the first sentence, the words **they** and **are** have been left out:

Most, if not all, people have certain things that **they** think **are** impossible to do.

Read the passage and decide where the other 17 missing words have been left out and write them on a piece of paper. It is better not to mark the text so that you can repeat the exercise. This is the kind of exercise you can do before you write an essay or before you check an essay.

The art of doing the impossible

Most, if not all, people have certain things that think impossible to do. Take dealing domestic chores. For some of us, summoning enough energy to tidy rooms or flats or sort out months of paper or to change the bed all require a lot of effort. At work, also, tackling even simplest tasks sometimes seems insurmountable as more complex jobs.

So it not exactly surprising that for many people stepping outside the limits of their experience or beliefs almost out of the question. It difficult to change people's habits and views of world. Yet, fortunately, there have been, and still are, individuals have influenced mankind, because they challenged tradition. Few of us dare to hold opinion has no currency within the teachings we have learnt. Original among our peers and family also sets us apart we then become targets of jealousy or envy. To develop outlook that is broader than one's friends or that is just different is dangerous, but it is something, which must encouraged if we are to develop. Wilde said that we all in the gutter, but some of us are gazing at the stars. In modern era, will the star-gazers prevail?

Exercise 12: checking in waves

This exercise gives you some specific help with checking your writing for different types of mistakes. The text below contains three kinds of mistake:

> A. 17 spelling mistakes
> B. 7 missing words
> C. 4 irrelevant pieces of information

Read through the text below as quickly as you can. Then look for each type of mistake separately.

Note: when you are checking spelling, do you need to read the text?

> Essay title:
>
> Should we be worried about making mistakes? Some people believe that we should avoid making mistakes of any kind in our lives. What is your position in this matter?

It good to make mistakes inspite of what some people might think. Many of us go through our lives in sheer teror of doing something wrong, becaus we have taught that every task should always be performed correctly. This is nonsence, however. This is obviously where teaching children comes in.

A good part of the problem, I feel, lies not with the mistakes themselves, but with labeling aspects of the learning process as errors rather seeing them as a natural, and neccesary, developement. Doing things in the wrong way should surely be avoided. Take children as an example. They have to fall down in order to learn to stand again; the same aplies to everything that they do, including mental tasks. If children at school or at home constantly harrassed about doing everything correctly, there is a good chance they will just give up. It is possible for them then to become afraid of openning themselves up to the censure of others. Yet, children need surely to make mistakes in order to see what is right and not to be constantly snapped at for failure.

Adults leaning to use new technology are also a case in point. Computers are able to check for spelling mistakes, which is a helpful tool. And what about learning to drive, which is also fun? Grown-ups may have dificulties mastering the process and make lots of mistakes, but those who concentrate on their failures rather than aquiring the skill they are trying to learn tend to give up. By contrast, those who focused on the task rather than their mistakes usually suceed.

And the solution? The simple answer is to trian people to treat mistakes and miner hiccups as natural steps in the process of learning. Teachers and trainers could point that, although students should aim to be perfect, they must realise that they are going to make mistakes and learn from them. This positive atitude will help build confidence and stop people giving up. On a general note, if people are constantly making mistakes, new discoveries will not be made.

Exercise 13: second wave

In this exercise, you have the same text as in the previous exercise. All the spelling is correct and there are no missing words. Without looking back at the previous exercise, find:

> A. 10 extra definite articles (the)
> B. 2 modal verbs which are wrong

It is good to make mistakes in spite of what some people should think. Many of us go through our lives in sheer terror of doing something wrong, because we have been taught that every task should always be performed correctly. This is nonsense, however.

A good part of the problem, I feel, lies not with the mistakes themselves, but with labelling the aspects of the learning process as errors rather than seeing them as a natural, and necessary, development. Take the children as an example. They have to fall down in order to learn to stand up again; the same applies to everything that they do, including mental tasks. If children at the school or at home are constantly harassed about doing everything correctly, there is a good chance they will just give up. It is possible for them then to become afraid of opening themselves up to the censure of others. Yet, the children need surely to make mistakes in order to see what is right and not to be constantly snapped at for failure.

Adults learning to use the new technology are also a case in point. Computers are able to check for spelling mistakes, which is a helpful tool. Grown-ups must have difficulties mastering the process and make lots of the mistakes, but those who concentrate on their failures rather than acquiring the skill they are trying to learn tend to give up. By contrast, those who are focused on the task rather than their mistakes usually succeed.

And the solution? The simple answer is to train the people to treat mistakes and the minor hiccups as natural steps in the process of learning. The teachers and trainers could point out that, although students should aim to be perfect, they must realise that they are going to make mistakes and learn from them. This positive attitude will help build the confidence and stop people giving up.

Exercise 14: prepositions at speed

Another area of language where candidates frequently make mistakes is when using prepositions. This is sometimes because a candidate does not know which preposition to use, but it also occurs, because candidates do not check their work.

Read the sentences below and decide whether the prepositions in each sentence are correct. If you think they are wrong, correct them. Some sentences may have no mistakes.

1. While I have considerable sympathy to this idea, there are certain aspects that I do not approve at.
2. At 2000, people were filled with new optimism.
3. It is not really sensible to rely on data, no matter where they come from.
4. There has been considerable improvement with the way business is conducted over the past few years.
5. The success for any venture depends in a host of variables.
6. The money should not be spent for weapons but for education, the infrastructure, etc.
7. Our attitude to work needs to change; otherwise, more jobs will be lost.
8. While this may be an advantage to some, a considerable number of people will see little benefit of it.
9. No country should interfere into the affairs of another nation.
10. Few people believe that the legalisation of soft drugs is an improvement on the current situation.
11. People's views for the subject are difficult to gauge.
12. Some people argue that there is no point of the government putting more money into public services unless efficiency is increased.
13. Although I object to some aspects of this argument, my views of this matter generally do not differ from the writer's.
14. Many qualified teachers are still lacking of basic skills and training.
15. It is well known that teenagers have enormous influence over each other.
16. There is a serious lack in qualified teachers in this field.
17. This is, however, dependent on certain criteria being fulfilled.
18. People in general do not think carefully enough of the consequences of their actions.
19. Some people, by contrast, are struggling daily in finding their basic needs in order to survive.
20. I largely agree on you with the above matter.
21. The government has succeeded to alienate the electorate very quickly.
22. The city council needs to think of this matter more carefully before it proceeds on the pedestrianisation of the centre.
23. The key to this problem is not as obvious as it first appears.

Exercise 15: language for graphs and charts etc - revision

In this and the following exercise, the sentences have been adapted from the first section on graphs and charts etc. Read the sentences carefully and see if you can find the mistakes. There may be more than one mistake per sentence. In the first sentence, for example, there are four errors.

Note that you need to look at all the information.

1. During October, visitors numbers fell off their september peek, they dropped over 40,000 visitors by the end of the year.

2. The data shows that the trend was obviuosly upwards.

3. Picking up numbers at 1999, it leapt considerably.

4. The improvement in year 2001 was marked by sells surge to 5 millions euros.

5.   Number of people visit the museum rised approximatly 30,000 a month throuhout the year 2000.

6.   The visitor numbers rise in July was gradual.

7.   In 2001, 20 millions copies of the book were sold.

8.   The steady increase in attendances from 30,000 to around 45,000 in the first four month followed by a sharper rise in May.

9.   In the year 1990, sales shot significantly.

10.   The map show the changes took place in the area spaning a peroid of 25 years.

11.   The airport considerably enlarged by the buying of two bits of land.

12.   In 1986, an expansion was build to the house.

13.   According to the table, show the % of women in govt posts in years 1960 to 2000.

14.   the trend was fairly erattic, with a 2% drop to 13% in 1965, and followed by a raise of 1% five year latter.

15.   By contrast, sales increased to 13%, doubled to 26 per cent by 1975.

Exercise 16: more revision for graphs and charts etc

In this exercise, the sentences have been adapted from the first section of the book on graphs and charts etc. Read the sentences carefully and see if you can find the mistakes. There may be more than one mistake per sentence.

1.   The bar chart show the presumed profits in thousands of dollars.

2.   Growth are expected to slow untill 2004, after which it estimated that they will even

3.   By contrast, it is forecasted that the sales of computer games will outstripped music CDs in the coming future.

4.   DIY sales will rise fitfuly, rising at rate of 10 percent per month.

5.   Sales are projected to remain steady for the remaining three years.

6.   Wyers Ltd is expected to make a lose of 2 million euro in it's first year of trading

7.   According to the chart, from 2007 until 2009 inclusive, the town expected to experience negative population growth.

8.   The population will fall down gradually over the next five years from 2010 to 2015.

9.   The people numbers will grow up with 20%.

10.   As far as hotel ocupancy rates, it is expected that over the period they will excede all expectations.

11.   Falling initialy by 10% in the last quarter of the year, growth in sales will pick next year.

12.   Thereafter, however, the population's growth in London will be anticipated to be much slower.

13.   After that sales went up and down wildly, first doubling to 400 units, and subsequently falling again to the march level. Those fluctuations followed by relatives stability.

14.   From this level, the number of motorcycles sold jumpt dramatically, hiting a peak of just under 100.

15.   This was followed by a sharp drop of about 80 % in the number of purchased videos.

Exercise 17: right place?

In the text below many, but not all, of the verbs in various forms are in the wrong place. Can you find the correct home for the verbs?

Some people **believe** that **using** comics to **tackle** children **to read** more **is** not a good way **to encourage** the problem of illiteracy. They **think** that the pictures **discourage** readers from **using** for themselves and so **thinking** comics **is** another step in the **reading** down of the educational process. However, nothing **should be encouraged** further from the truth. Anything, comics included, which **induces** children, or indeed adults, **could be to read**. For my own part, I **are released** to some of the classic tales through picture books **telling** stories as indeed **were** many of my friends. **soar** the example of films **made** on books. When such films **was introduced** the sales of the books invariably **Take**. The same **applies** to books **based** into TV series. With comics, it **are** really no different. They **is** just one step away from **dumbing** a book. …

Exercise 18: connection revision

The passage below is taken from the second section of the book. Read through the text and you will be able to understand the writer's ideas, but you will not be able to see clearly how they fit together. Each section marked 2-14 has a problem relating to connection in the text. Improve or correct the connections.

Note that you may have to change the punctuation and add or delete words. Make as few changes to the text as possible. Note there are no spelling/grammar mistakes etc.

1. **Sport has a wide range of benefits.** 2. First, at an international level, football encourages people from different cultures to come into contact with each other. 3. Which then helps to break down barriers between different countries, 4. but furthers international cooperation. 5. For example, amateur sports meetings between schools and universities in different parts of the world. 6. Many countries arrange contacts, 7. because people at different levels in their respective societies develop closer bonds, 8. namely cultural exchanges or trade links. 9. It is obviously of mutual benefit to all concerned.

10. While some people are reluctant to take up any kind of sporting activity. 11. There is, however, overwhelming evidence that playing sport can have a very positive effect on health. 12. Activity improves coordination and, on the other hand, increases well-being. 13. It helps fight against disease. 14. Enhancing the quality of people's lives.

Exercise 19: punctuation check

Candidates sometimes do not realise that punctuation in their writing is important. In the paragraph below all of the punctuation marks are in the wrong place and so the text is nonsense. Therefore, you need to move the punctuation marks around the text to make it read sense. Note that you will have to remove and add capital letters as you move full stops.

> Example: the comma after the word *right* in the first line should be after the word *Admittedly,* and the full stop after *sure* should be after the word *purposes* in the second line. You should then remove the capital letter in the word *that* and put a capital letter at the beginning of the word *Whilst.*

Admittedly employers do have the right, to make sure. That the people who work for them are not using their work time for their own purposes whilst it is impossible to deny the truth of this, opinion I personally feel that the invasion of an individuals' privacy by, allowing employers to check on employees e-mail's and electronic work is, unacceptable employers. Can now track. every piece of work done. for example they can check everything, workers do on their computers what :work they have done what games; they have played what; they have looked at. On the internet they can also check whether the e-mails are related to their work. Or whether they are private surely all, of this amounts to an invasion of the individuals privacy'

Exercise 20: agreement and singular and plural

Some of the sentences below are correct and some have problems with singular and plural or agreement between subject and verb.

You cannot add or remove any words except to change a pronoun, e.g. **it** to **them** or a singular verb to a plural e.g. **is** to **are**.

Look at sentence 1:

There **is**, however, several reason**s** why the situation **need** to be dealt with as a soon as possible.

Is there anything you would like to change?

1. There is, however, several reasons why the situation need to be dealt with as a soon as possible.
2. Many people evidently agree with this point of views.
3. These new toys, which come on the market at regular intervals, puts enormous pressure on parent with young childrens.

4. Few are able to understand the complexity of this concept, but it do not mean that it should be ignored.

5. Beautiful surroundings are important for people's sense of well-being.

6. The computer, whether in the field of works or in the home, are the source of as much good as they are of harm.

7. Being in beautiful surroundings are important for one's sense of well-being.

8. Self-awareness do not as a rule come easily to everyone.

9. As far as safety and comfort on public transport is concerned, there is surely no room for equivocation on the part of the powers that be.

10. More attention than necessary have been devoted to this issue already.

11. In recent year, people have been more willing to accept greater stress at work than previously.

12. The future of the car industry is certainly secure, because people will always want to travel by private transport rather than a public system which are at the mercy of lack of funding and poor management.

13. At first glance, it would appear that all the available avenues has been exhausted, but there are a raft of measures that can be implemented.

14. The growth of e-mail and the increasing flexibility of employers means many people are turning to tele-working.

15. More than one in four of the workforce now works from home.

16. About two thirds of the workforce in this field are woman.

17. We must ask ourself whether it is acceptable for money to be poured into the arts when so many people are living below the poverty lines.

18. European painters such as Leonardo da Vinci, Raphael, Van Gogh etc is often more widely known than more contemporary artist.

19. The use of mobile phones are spreading rapidly among young people.

20. Politician need to put greater effort into sorting out the mess in the education world.

21. Another problem here are the cost to the poor, once the measure have been introduced.

22. Informations like advice depend largely on the experience of those that one obtains them from.

23. The government are now in a quandary over this situation.

24. There are little to choose between the two answers.

Section 4

Practice Writing Tests

CONTENTS

Page

Section 4 Practice writing tests

Test 1

Writing Task 1

You should spend about 20 minutes on this task.

The bar chart below shows a survey of a group of young professionals aged 20–30 years who were asked to state which factors motivated them to succeed.

Write a report for a university lecturer describing the information shown below.

You should write at least 150 words.

Factors motivating people to succeed

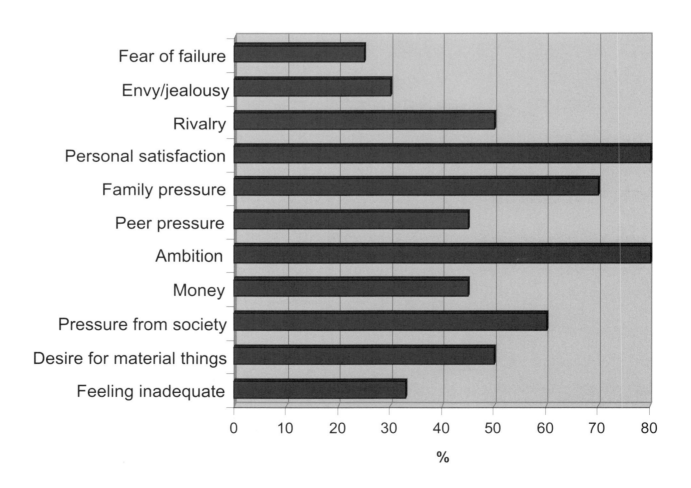

Writing Task 2

You should spend about 40 minutes on this task.

Present a written argument or case to an educated reader with no specialist knowledge of the following topic:

More and more qualified people are moving from poor to rich countries to fill vacancies in specialist areas like engineering, computing and medicine. Some people believe that by encouraging the movement of such people rich countries are stealing from poor countries. Others feel that this is only part of the natural movement of workers around the world.

♦ What is your opinion?
♦ Do you think rich countries should pay poorer countries for the people they encourage to come?
♦ What other measures could rich countries take to encourage qualified people to stay and help develop their own countries?

You should write at least 250 words.

Use your own ideas, knowledge and experience and support your arguments with examples and with relevant evidence.

Test 2

Writing Task 1

You should spend about 20 minutes on this task.

The bar chart below shows the results of a poll of theatre-goers on what disturbs them during performances at the theatre.

Write a report for a university lecturer describing the information shown below.

You should write at least 150 words.

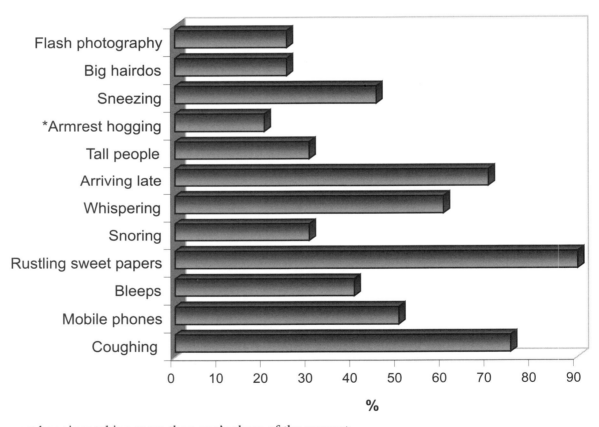

Irritants for theatre-goers

*Armrest hogging: taking more than one's share of the armrest

Writing Task 2

You should spend about 40 minutes on this task.

Present a written argument or case to an educated reader with no specialist knowledge of the following topic:

One day the world's oil and gas reserves will run out. The search for alternative energy sources like wind power, solar power, burning waste, and water power are causing as much environmental damage as the oil and nuclear power sources they are intended to replace.

··   How far do you agree with this latter statement?
··   What possible benefits do the alternative energy sources bring? **OR** What damage do they cause?

You should write at least 250 words.

Use your own ideas, knowledge and experience and support your arguments with examples and with relevant evidence.

Test 3

Writing Task 1

You should spend about 20 minutes on this task.

The graph below shows the value in thousands of dollars of three companies selling farming equipment every five years from 1960 and their projected value from 2007 to 2012. Farm Implements Ltd did not start trading until 1980.

Write a report for a university lecturer describing the information shown below.

You should write at least 150 words.

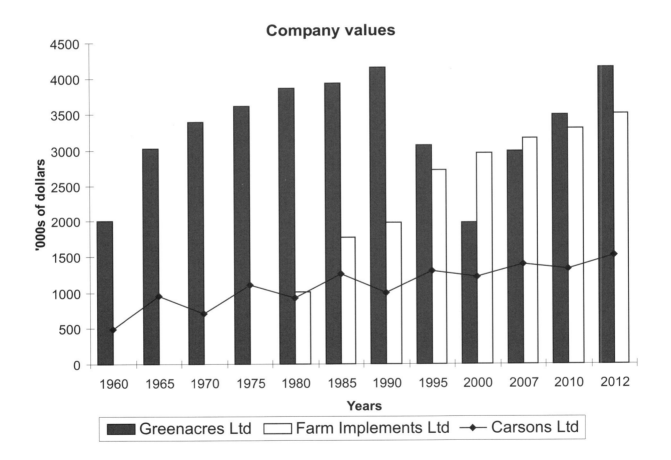

Writing Task 2

You should spend about 40 minutes on this task.

Present a written argument or case to an educated reader with no specialist knowledge of the following topic:

Only formal examinations, written or practical, can give a clear picture of students' true knowledge and ability at university level. Continuous assessment like course work and projects are poor measures of student ability.

♦   How far do you agree with this latter statement?

You should write at least 250 words.

Use your own ideas, knowledge and experience and support your arguments with examples and with relevant evidence.

Test 4

Writing Task 1

You should spend about 20 minutes on this task.

The table below shows the percentage of pupils who entered higher education from five secondary schools between 1995 and 2000 inclusive.

Write a report for a university lecturer describing the information shown below.

You should write at least 150 words.

Years	Royston Academy	Greystone High	Harble Secondary	Fairfield Girls	Crackend Boys
1995	50	90	30	65	60
1996	52	80	35	70	59
1997	54	75	40	75	60
1998	54	73	50	75	61
1999	60	72	60	70	60
2000	60	70	80	79	62

Writing Task 2

You should spend about 40 minutes on this task.

Present a written argument or case to an educated reader with no specialist knowledge of the following topic:

Although tourists in many countries are a significant source of revenue, they are frowned upon for various reasons. For the tourist, however, travelling is supposed to broaden the mind and be an educational experience.

◆   In what ways do you think travelling does this?
◆   And in what ways do you think travelling does the opposite, i.e. narrows people minds?

You should write at least 250 words.

Use your own ideas, knowledge and experience and support your arguments with examples and with relevant evidence.

Test 5

Writing Task 1

You should spend about 20 minutes on this task.

The diagram below shows the results of a survey of a sample of 1,000 people on the different sources of noise which cause a nuisance. The severity of the nuisance is measured on a scale running from *Not annoying* to *Extremely annoying*.

Write a report for a university lecturer describing the information shown below.

You should write at least 150 words.

Not annoying	Fairly annoying	Annoying	Very annoying	Extremely annoying

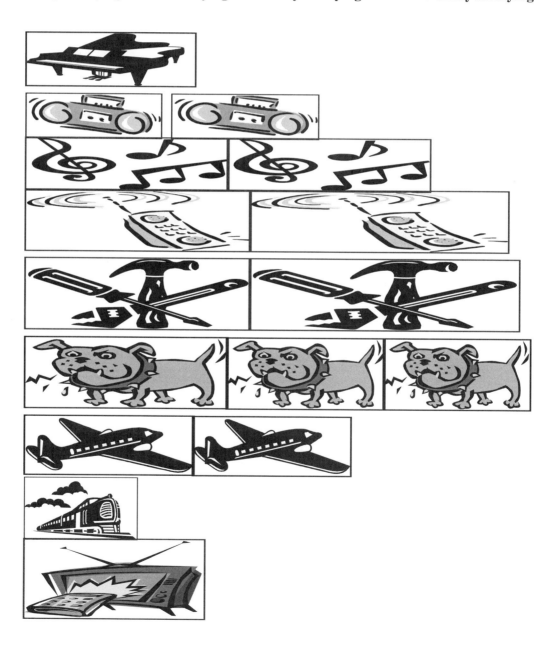

Writing Task 2

You should spend about 40 minutes on this task.

Present a written argument or case to an educated reader with no specialist knowledge of the following topic:

As populations grow and cities become more crowded, there is pressure throughout the world to construct ever taller buildings to provide accommodation and offices. Many people object to such developments, citing the social as well as the physical dangers.

♦   What benefits do skyscrapers bring?
♦   Do you agree with the objections to skyscrapers?

You should write at least 250 words.

Use your own ideas, knowledge and experience and support your arguments with examples and with relevant evidence.

Test 6

Writing Task 1

You should spend about 20 minutes on this task.

The maps below show the changes in the size of West Farm and in the value of the land per hectare over a period of 90 years from 1900 to 1990.

Write a report for a university lecturer describing the information shown below.

You should write at least 150 words.

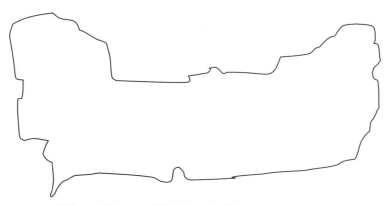

West Farm 1900 – 5,000 hectares
Value per hectare: 1 dollar

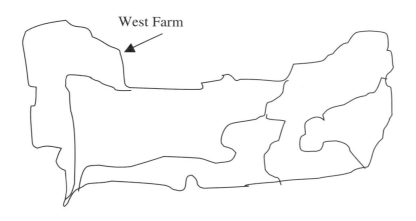

West Farm

West Farm 1925 – 850 hectares
Value per hectare: 20 dollars

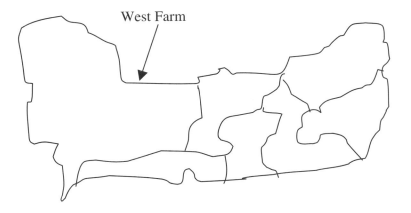

West Farm 1940 – 1700 hectares
Value per hectare: 25 dollars

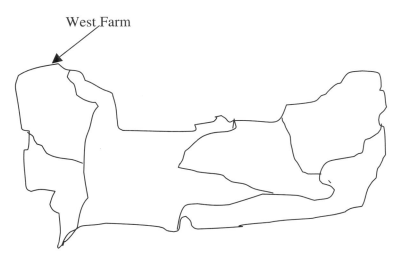

West Farm 1970 – 500 hectares
Value per hectare: 100 dollars

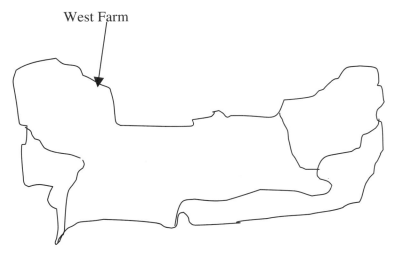

West Farm 1990 – 3,500 hectares
Value per hectare: 125 dollars

Writing Task 2

You should spend about 40 minutes on this task.

Present a written argument or case to an educated reader with no specialist knowledge of the following topic:

Trees are essential for the existence of the human race as they provide the oxygen that we need to survive. Yet, daily all around the globe large areas of woodland are being destroyed. Many people feel that they as individuals can do nothing and that only governments and large companies can halt the destruction.

♦ How far do you agree or disagree with this?

Use your own ideas, knowledge and experience and support your arguments with examples and with relevant evidence.

Test 7

Writing Task 1

You should spend about 20 minutes on this task.

The charts below show part of the results of an extensive public survey on people's attitude to a range of issues.

Write a report for a university lecturer describing the information shown below.

You should write at least 150 words.

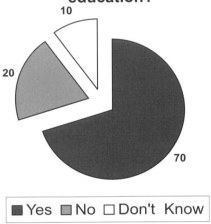

Do you think more money should be invested in education?

10

20

70

■ Yes ■ No □ Don't Know

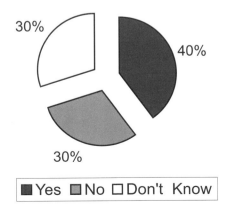

Do you think more money should be invested in health than education?

30%

40%

30%

■ Yes ■ No □ Don't Know

Do you think more money should be invested in public transport rather than education?

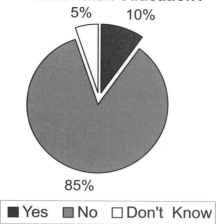

5% 10%

85%

■ Yes ■ No □ Don't Know

Do you think taxes should be raised to pay for public services such as education, health and public transport?

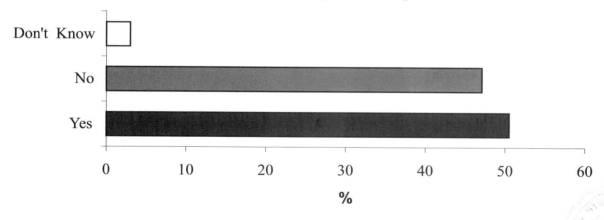

Writing Task 2

You should spend about 40 minutes on this task.

Present a written argument or case for an educated reader with no specialist knowledge of the following topic:

In the future, we will have more and more leisure time as machines replace many of the tasks we do at home and at work. Discuss the benefits this will bring and also the problems it will cause.

You should write at least 250 words.

Use your own ideas, knowledge and experience and support your arguments with examples and with relevant evidence.

Test 8

Writing Task 1

You should spend about 20 minutes on this task.

The table below shows the percentage of the rooms occupied in six hotels during May to September between 1985 and 2000. The table also indicates the star rating of each hotel.

Write a report for a university lecturer describing the information shown below.

You should write at least 150 words.

	Stars	1985	1990	1995	2000
Hotel Concorde	*****	90	90	30	65
Hamilton's	*****	100	100	95	70
The Tower	****	57	85	55	85
Hotel Olivia	***	90	85	89	95
Hampton's	***	100	100	90	100
The Continental	***	79	83	70	80

Writing Task 2

You should spend about 40 minutes on this task.

Present a written argument or case to an educated reader with no specialist knowledge of the following topic:

The Internet is becoming more and more central to our lives, as it provides more and more information, acts as interactive entertainment, and as a means of voting, etc. These functions have obvious benefits, but there are dangers involved in the control the Internet is exerting over our lives.

◆ What benefits are involved?
◆ What dangers are involved?
◆ How far do you agree or disagree with the opinion expressed?

You should write at least 250 words.

Use your own ideas, knowledge and experience and support your arguments with examples and with relevant evidence.

Test 9

Writing Task 1

You should spend about 20 minutes on this task.

The chart below shows the actual and estimated number of visitors to a new art gallery from its opening date in 1990 up to and including 2001. It also indicates three events in the gallery's life. Below the chart there are two pie charts which show the Satisfaction rating of visitors to the gallery in 1990 and 2001.

Write a report for a university lecturer describing the information shown below.

You should write at least 150 words.

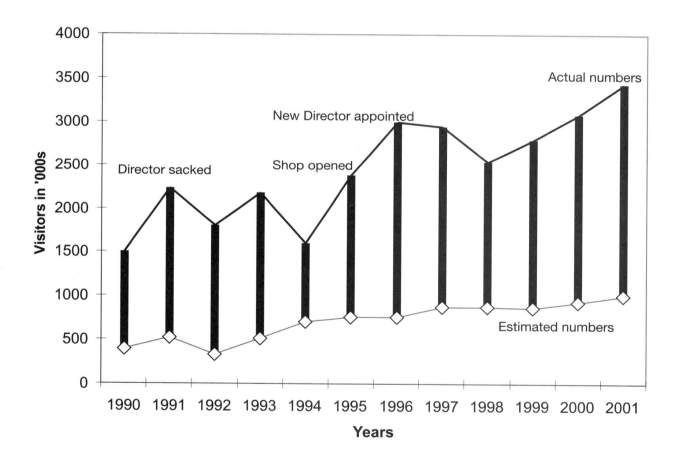

Satisfaction rating in 1990

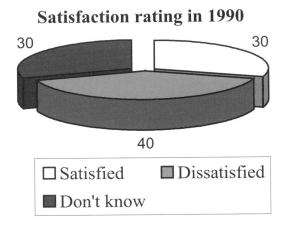

30   30

40

☐ Satisfied   ▨ Dissatisfied

■ Don't know

Satisfaction rating in 2001

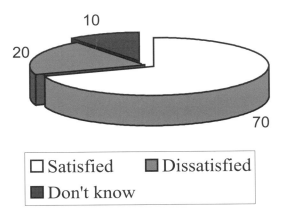

10

20

70

☐ Satisfied   ▨ Dissatisfied

■ Don't know

Writing Task 2

You should spend about 40 minutes on this task.

Present a written argument or case to an educated reader with no specialist knowledge of the following topic:

High technology is now being harnessed to help the elderly by providing monitoring, tracking and, perhaps, one day robots as companions. Whilst there are obvious benefits for the elderly in these developments, some people are uneasy about the social consequences.

♦   What are the negative consequences?
♦   What is your opinion on the matter?

You should write at least 250 words.

Use your own ideas, knowledge and experience and support your arguments with examples and with relevant evidence.

Test 10

Writing Task 1

You should spend about 20 minutes on this task.

The graph below shows the Satisfaction rating of the staff in four colleges from 1991 to 2002.

Write a report for a university lecturer describing the information shown below.

You should write at least 150 words.

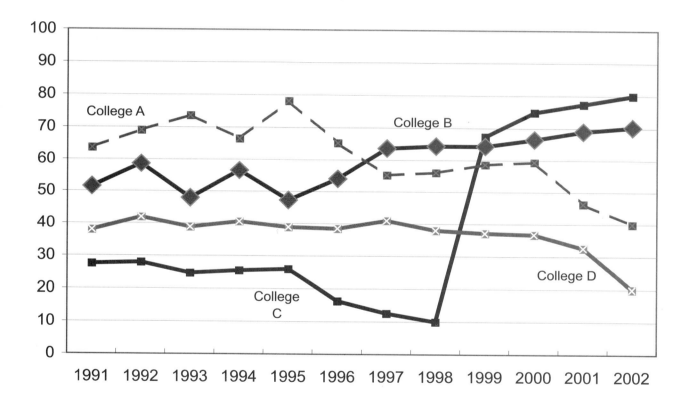

Writing Task 2

You should spend about 40 minutes on this task.

Present a written argument or case to an educated reader with no specialist knowledge of the following topic:

The wealth of a nation is said to depend on the health of its citizens. Yet, in the modern knowledge-based economies of the world, education is more and more being seen as the main force in the development of all countries.

♦   Do you share this view?
♦   Are there other factors involved? If so, which?

You should write at least 250 words.

Use your own ideas, knowledge and experience and support your arguments with examples and with relevant evidence.

Key
to
Section 1

Exercise 1

1. False	7. True	12. True
2. True	8. False	13. False
3. False	9. True	14. False
4. True	10. True	15. True
5. False	11. False. Note the phrase	
6. True	*just short of*.	

Note how some of the sentences are general statements, e.g. 2, 6, 8, etc. Others contain specific detail, e.g. 3, 4, 5, 7, etc. Statement 1, however, starts off generally and ends with specific information.

Exercise 2

♦ The number of books sold was fairly steady over the first few weeks of the year with a slight rise to 200 per day. **[A]**

♦ After that sales went up and down wildly, first doubling to 400 units, **[D]**

♦ and subsequently falling back erratically again to 200 books. **[C]**

♦ These fluctuations were followed by a period of stability as sales hovered around the 200 mark. **[E]**

♦ Book purchases, however, proved very erratic again, but the trend was upward this time, reaching the 400 per day level. **[D]**

♦ The number of books sold then plunged dramatically, hitting a low of 100, only to bounce back to 500 books a day. **[I]**

♦ The recovery was short-lived, however, as sales fell back again to 200 **[B]**

♦ around which they remained for a short time **[E]**

♦ before climbing again, albeit fitfully to 400. **[D]**

♦ Book sales then plummeted to a new low of 50 a day where they stabilised for a period before shooting up again to the 600 mark. **[G]**

♦ This was followed by a sharp drop of approximately 80 % in the number of books purchased. **[H]**

Notice:

♦ the variety in the noun phrases used to avoid repetition: *The number of books sold/ sales/ books/ sales/ Book purchases/ The number of books sold/ sales/ Book sales/ sales/ the number of books purchased.*

♦ repetition is not about avoiding the same word altogether, but alternating it with other words and phrases

♦ the other attempts to avoid repeating the same words, e.g. *hovered, remained, stabilised* and *the sales went up and down ...... these fluctuations ... .*

Compare Exercise 10.

Exercise 3

1. C.	6. F.	11. B.	16. K
2. Q.	7. A.	12. H.	17. J.
3. E.	8. I.	13. L.	18. O.
4. M.	9. R	14. P.	19. S.
5. D.	10. N	15. G.	

As in Exercise 2, notice how the passage avoids repetition through phrases like: *the number of houses built/ the number of houses that were erected/ new house construction*. What other words and phrases can you find?

Exercise 4

1. With this kind of bar chart there is no trend. The items listed can be compared by putting them into groups or categories, if it is possible to do so.

2. The horizontal axis lists the factors about which the survey sample was questioned. The vertical axis gives the percentage of the sample who cited the factors as causing stress. It is worth noting that the percentages do not add up to 100%, as in a pie chart. Also members of the sample are likely to have quoted more than one factor. For example, in the case of Getting divorced 600 people said that this was a stress factor, whereas 300 people cited Noise problems. We do not know if the latter 300 all quoted Getting divorced as a factor or whether 150/120 or none quoted it.

3. Because the factor with the highest percentage does not go above 80%. So there is no need to go up to 100%. This is common in graphs and bar charts.

4. You could put the factors into three groups those that are <u>work related</u>: *Getting to work, New technology, Work related worries;* those <u>that are family related</u>: *Getting divorced, Children's future, Home security, Moving house, Problems with neighbours and Noise problems*; and <u>personal</u> factors: *Worries about own future*. You could put *Getting divorced* into the last group. You could also have other groups.

5. By putting the factors into these groups, it is easier to compare and contrast the factors. You can compare the groups and you can compare the items within each group and across groups.

6. You could write: *Of the adults polled, more than 70% cited Moving house as the main stress factor.* **Or** *Among the factors relating to the home and family, Moving house was the highest at over 70%.* **Or** *Moving house was given by more than 70% of those polled as causing the most stress.* There are also other ways.

7. You could write: *The stress factor with the lowest rating in all three categories was Problems with neighbours at approximately 15% of the sample.* **Or** you could write: *Problems with neighbours is/was/ are/were rated/given/cited/mentioned/quoted as the factor creating the least stress at approximately 15% of the sample.*

8. There are not many words that you could use as alternatives here, you could have: *contributing factor; cause; reason for; reason why; source of.*

9. They should read:

   ♦ *...was/is cited... ; were/are cited.* It depends whether you consider *Worries ...* as an item or a plural word. The tense depends on whether you look at the chart as it is now or as the result of a past survey.

   ♦ *... Work related worries as a factor....*

   ♦ *... 40 per cent of those sampled .....*

10. The information is organised in different ways in each sentence. If all of your sentences have the same pattern, the examiner will think that your range of grammar is limited. It is not enough just to have a range of vocabulary. In the first sentence, the percentage is the subject of the verb: *30% ... cite worries*

about the future of their children. In the second, *worries* is the subject. In the third sentence, *30%* is again the subject and *stress* the object. There is a further difference worth noting. The verb in 10a is in the present tense and the others are in the past. You can talk about charts like this in the present, as you are looking at them as a fact now. You can also talk about them in the past as the survey has already been conducted. Note that the verb *cite* is in the plural.

11. *...cause(d) stress; are/were quoted/cited as a cause of/ as causing stress/ as a contributing factor to stress.*

12. It is generally easier to describe trends and changes from one time to another. Also the items on bar charts like this are sometimes difficult to use in sentences as they tend to make long noun phrases as in 9 above. Note also that here the writer has used capitals to quote the items on the chart, e.g. *Moving house*, but when putting the items into a sentence as in 10a above, remember you are not quoting the item directly: *...cite worries about the future of their children* ..... You are putting the item into the grammar of the sentence and capitals are not necessary. You may also find that the different items in charts are presented with or without capitals or all in capitals.

Exercise 5

1. February
2. February to April
3. February to April
4. May, August, May
5. January
6. January, April; February, April
7. May
8. June; August
9. May; November; December
10. August December
11. August

This exercise like the previous ones makes you interact with the chart so that you can relate to graphs etc more easily.

Exercise 6

1. J
2. F
3. D
4. E
5. H
6. I
7. B
8. C
9. A
10. K
11. G

Note how you can predict the next part of the text using the grammar. For example, 2. F (... TV and ...) ; 3. D (...all four ...; 4. E (... people ... play ...); 5. H (... **in** Reading, 25% **in** ...) and so on.

Exercise 7

1. 20 years of age.

2. When he was about 25 years of age.

3. 100 years of age.

4. From his mid-twenties to the age of 70; from his early 80s until he died at 100.

5. In his early 40s.

6. After they were published for the first time, none of their writing went unpublished.

7. The novelist.

8. They both died at the age of 100.

9. He wrote for a longer period than the others before his work was published - between the ages of 20 and approximately 55; he was the only one who died while his work was not being published; he had the shortest publication time; he died before the others.

10. You could put the two academics together and the novelist and sci-fi writer together. Or you could put the Sci-fi writer and the two academics together in one group.

11. The first group in 10 is logical because of the type of writing. The second group is logical because of the nature of their published work. The publication record of the Novelist is noticeably different from the other three.

Exercise 8

A. ThamesMart
B. FineMmart
C. TewkesMart
D. '000s of euros
E. daily sales (figures)
F. percentage

G. TewkesMart
H. 17
I. Electrical
J. 20
K. Computer
L. 13

M. 10
N. 20
O. Toys

Exercise 9

1. FinGroup Ltd
2. Man Ltd
3. Bluebird Ltd
4. Man Ltd
5. FinGroup Ltd
6. FinGroup Ltd
7. FinGroup Ltd
8. Man Ltd
9. Bluebird Ltd

10. FinGroup Ltd
11. Man Ltd
12. Bluebird Ltd
13. Man Ltd
14. FinGroup Ltd
15. FinGroup Ltd
16. Man Ltd

Exercise 10

1. In 2001, there were wild fluctuations in personal computer sales at VH Warehouse.

2. During the three-year period, there was an obvious downward trend/trend downward.

3. Picking up again in the first quarter of 2000, sales rocketed by more than 100%.

4. There was a marked improvement in computer sales in the first quarter of 2000 with a surge of more than 100% [or with a more than 100% surge]. **Or** There was a marked improvement in the first quarter of 2000 with computer sales surging more than 100%.

5. From the first quarter of 2000 through to the first quarter of 2001, there was a fall of at least 1,000 in the number of computers sold quarterly. **Or** ... there was a fall in the number of computers sold quarterly of at least 1,000.

6. PC sales declined gradually during the first three quarters of 1999.

7. After falling gradually from 14,000 to approximately 6,000 in the first four quarters, quarterly computer sales increased sharply in the first quarter of 2000 to 12,000.

8. Between the first quarter of 2000 and the first quarter of 2001, sales decreased at a much slower pace than in 1999.

9. Over the year as a whole, there was a significant decrease in computer purchases
10. In the third quarter of 2001, there was a dramatic jump in the volume of sales.
11. Declining dramatically to around 2,000 machines in the second quarter of 2001, computer sales suddenly leapt to 8,000 in the third quarter.
12. After soaring in the first quarter of 2000, purchases then fell back again the following month

Exercise 11

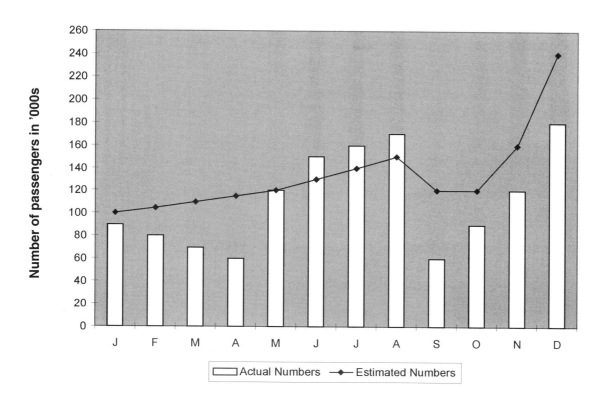

Exercise 12

1. viii

2. ix
3. x
4. –
5. xiii (Note that to avoid the repetition of the word *receive* in the first paragraph, it is better to use *takes* here.)
6. –

7. –
8. xii
9. iv
10. –
11. xi (It is better to use *handles* here in order to avoid the repetition of the word *take*. See 8 above.)
12. ii

13. –
14. iii
15. –
16. xv
17. vi
18. xvii
19. vii
20. i
21. xiv.

Exercise 13

Read the text and find where the words and phrases have been added. The first one has been done for you

The pie charts show the market share of washing machines **made by** four companies over the period 1990 to 2000 and the results of a survey on whether customers would consider buying the new Dyton washing machine over the same period.

During the first year of sales of the new Dyton machine in 1990, its market share stood at 2 percent as opposed to 60 percent for the MMC product, 20 for the Corr washing machine and 18 for that of Obecalp. In 1995, however, MMC Ltd lost ground to its three other competitors. While Corr Ltd and Obecalp Ltd both increased their market share to by one percentage point each in 1995, Dyton Ltd captured 8% of the market, a rise of 300%.

In 2000, Dyton's market share had increased to 32% at the expense of its three main competitors with MMC Ltd, Obecalp Ltd and Corr Ltd falling to 39 percent, 17 percent and 12 percent respectively.

The bar chart shows that the Dyton machine exceeded its popularity rating in each year, rising from 5 in 1995 to 40 percent in the year 2000.

It is clear that the sales of the Dyton washing machine were on the increase over the period.

Exercise 14

As you build the text, you can use the grammar to predict the next section you need. When you are writing a similar process is taking place.

Paragraph 1: E I F P D H R M G B C N A J O Q K L
Paragraph 2: U V T S Y W X

Exercise 15

1. A. Alternative A avoids the repetition in B and gives more information than D. As for C, using the noun here feels awkward, and it repeats the beginning sentence.
2. A. Alternative B is not correct, because it is not a matter of losing people (that you cannot find); in C the word *down* is wrong; and D is too informal.
3. A. Alternatives B, C and D are repetitive. Also using the preposition *with* followed by a noun is more sophisticated.
4. D. The other alternatives mean the same and are correct grammatically, but do not express the information quite so neatly.
5. B. See 1C. As you concentrate on the immediate text, it is easy to forget words that have been used before. The word *prediction* is not that far away!
6. B.
7. B/C. Both are correct and B might be better if you wanted to avoid the repetition of the construction *with + noun* as in 3A. A is possible, but not as good as the other two. Note the repetition in D of *forecast*- see 5B.
8. A. Note the repetition in B. The word *say* in C is not suitable here. The word *predict* in A is okay here as it is now a long way from the first sentence.
9. B. Note the grammar of the other alternatives.
10. D. Note the grammar in relation to the previous section of text.
11. C. Alternative D is possible, but A/B are less likely as you would need the word *and* at the beginning.
12. B.
13. D.

Exercise 16

The changes are marked in bold.

The bar chart shows the **predicted** profits for next year in thousands of **euros** for three companies, two of which will not start trading until **April**.

Tardy's profits are forecast to come in at the **100,000** level in January and are then expected to remain there until **March**, following which it is estimated that they will shoot up **sevenfold** in one month, to 700,000 euros in **April**. After a modest rise in May to 800,000 euros, profits are set to remain **stable** for the rest of the year.

By contrast, it is projected that the profit for Martfirst will operate at a loss of 100,000 euros in the first month of trade in **April**. Thereafter, however, there is anticipated to be a steady increase in profits, which will climb at the rate of **200,000** euros per month until they reach 800,000 euros in August. Profits will then remain steady for the rest of the year.

As regards Finenet Ltd, a loss of 300 000 euros is expected in its first month of trading, but then from May to **September**, profits will climb quickly to 1 million euros, before falling back **slightly** in the subsequent three months.

As can be seen, the overall trends for the three companies are upward.

Exercise 17

The full text is as follows:

The bar chart shows the results of a performance assessment by the colleagues and subordinates of four managers. In the assessment, the performance of the four managers was rated on a percentage scale.

One of the most striking features of the chart is the ratings scored by Mr Chandra, who consistently achieved 70% or above in all categories with the highest being the Ability to command respect at 90% and the lowest, Management flair, at 70%. Mr Chandra also came out top in seven out of the eight categories

Mr Forrest, however, was at the opposite end of the scale. Out of the eight categories, he scored only 10% in five, managing to gain higher ratings in only three categories, of which the top was 50% for General appearance. For the other two, Punctuality and Staff management, Mr Forrest gained 30% and 15%, respectively.

Of the other two managers, Mrs Monroe's scores ranged from 80%, her highest rating, for Punctuality to 5% for General appearance, the lowest of all four managers in this category. Likewise, Mrs Whitbread scored in the range of 70% for Organisational ability to 30% for Staff management.

Exercise 18

1. of changes took place
2. plots of land enlarged the garden/made the garden larger.
3. adjacent to the southern border was bought
4. almost equalled. [Note the word *and* connects two main verbs *was bought* and *equalled*. Note the tense in the second paragraph. You could write the whole text in the present.]
5. was effectively doubled by the
6. another/a plot (of land)
7. was extended on the southern side
8. planting of an orchard
9. added to the garden
10. a vegetable garden [was added]
11. lines of trees were planted [Maybe, to avoid the repetition of the word *plant* (see 8 above) in this version you could use *erected* here.]

Exercise 19

	Macrohard Ltd	Barnes Ltd	Eastman Ltd
	%	%	%
1960	2	8	15
1965	2	10	13
1970	13	12	14
1975	26	14	21
1985	32	16	19
2000	63	45	25

Please note the following:

Avoidance of repetition:

Note how the text tries to avoid using the same verb each time. Note also that the verb *held* is repeated, but the second is far away from the first use of the word and it is passive, whereas the first is active.

- ◆ … more women were in senior positions …
- ◆ … women held 7% more top management jobs than in 1970.
- ◆ … top posts were filled by women …
- ◆ … 2% of senior posts were occupied by women …
- ◆ … there was a 6% increase in female senior management jobs …
- ◆ … the percentage of senior posts held by women was 8% …

General to specific

The trend was fairly erratic [General], with a 2% drop to 13% in 1965, followed by a rise of 1% five years later. [Specific]

Comparison and contrast

Note the different ways that comparison and contrast are used in the text.

♦ While at Eastman Ltd … than the two companies in 1960 at 15. In 1975.
♦ After a slight drop back to 19% in 1985, by 2000 25% of …
♦ …women held 7% more top management jobs than in 1970.
♦ By contrast, at Macrohard Ltd women fared much better.
♦ … 63%, the highest for the three companies.
♦ The situation was less remarkable at Barnes Ltd than the other two firms except for the year 2000.

Exercise 20

Text	1. A	2. A	3. C	4. B	5. C	6. B	7. A

Pictures	1. J	2. I	3. A	4. D	5. C	6. H	7. E
	8. B	9. G	10. F	11. J			

Key
to
Section 2

Exercise 1

1. a
2. b. Note that this is theoretical possibility. We do not know whether it will be built or not.
3. b. Compare number 2. This is practical possibility: It is physically possible to build the motorway.
4. d
5. c
6. d; c, if it is true then it is also a fact.
7. b
8. c. Note that some people may call also this a probability. Compare number 9.
9. c. Compare 8c.
10. b
11. b/d
12. b
13. d. If you replace the exclamation mark with a full-stop, this sentence becomes a past possibility
14. a/d
15. a
16. c
17. c
18. a/c
19. a. The word criminal indicates the writer's opinion.

Exercise 2

1. (c) a result. Note the relationship: condition/result.
2. (a) a result. Note the relationship: condition/result. Also note how the verb + ing is used to give the result.
3. (a) examples/(b) an explanation. Note how the text in italics explains how young people are to be encouraged. There are two examples.
4. (b) a proposal. Note the relationship here: reason/proposal.
5. (c) a concession. The contrast is in the other part of the sentence.
6. (b) a reason
7. (a) an example/(c) a tentative proposal
8. (d) a condition
9. (a) a reason. Note how the reason is expressed: *Being aware* .... Compare numbers 6 and 11.
10. (a) a contrast
11. (c) a reason. Note how the reason is expressed: *Knowing* .... Compare numbers 6 and 9.
12. (a) a conclusion.
13. (b) a concession. Note how the concession is expressed: ...*may* ..., *but* .... Compare number 5 above.

Note how a result is expressed in different ways: compare sentences 1, 2 and 8 (the main clause). Compare also the different ways that reasons are expressed in sentences 6, 9 and 11. Note also the different ways concessions are expressed in sentences 5 and 13.

Exercise 3

1. (a) a proposal/(b) a recommendation;
   (d) a reason/(e) a result
2. (c) a purpose;
   (a) a proposal/(b) a recommendation
3. (a) an opinion/(b) a measure;
   (c) an explanation/(d) a reason
4. (a) a suggestion;
   (c) a tentative result/(d) an effect
5. (a) a suggestion;
   (b) a result/(d) an effect
6. (a) a suggestion;
   (c) a purpose
7. (b) an obligation;
   (d) a result
8. (b) a conclusion (e) a cause;
   (c) an effect
9. (b) a concession:
   (a) a contrast
10. (d) a reason (e) a cause;
    (b) an effect (c) a result
11. (d) a reason (e) a cause;
    (b) an effect (c) a result
12. (a) a reason;
    (c) an expectation

13. (a) a concession;
    (c) a contrast
14. b) a general statement;
    (a) an explanation
15. (b) a general statement;
    (d) an example

Exercise 4

If you find the exercise difficult, check some of the answers in the key. Then leave it and try it again another time. The sentence pairs are as follows:

- 1/18 or 18/1
- 2/14
- 13/3
- 4/11 or 11/4
- 21/5
- 22/6

- 7/19
- 8/16
- 9/17 or 17/9
- 20/12 or 12/20
- 10/15 or 15/10

Note how it is possible to write some of the sentences in a different order.

Exercise 5

Remember the sentences in each pair should have the same meaning.

1. *Example: A (xiii) moreover*
   Example: B (xvii) as well as
2. A (vi) although (xviii) though [(xxii) is awkward here because of *While what ...*]
   B (xvi) but. You cannot use *although* or *though* here.
3. A (x) although ...yet
   B (xiv) even so (xxi) nevertheless (xi) however. The word *however* here is not as strong as the first two and probably does not have the force of *although ... yet* in A.
4. A (xv) so that
   B (xix) in order to
5. A (ii) much as (vi) although (xviii) though (xxii) while
   B (xxiii) despite

6. A (i) otherwise
   B (xx) so as not
7. A (xi) however (xiv) even so (xxi) nevertheless
   B (xvi) but (vi) although (xviii) though
8. A (xviii) though (ix) as
   B (vi) although (xviii) though (xxii) while
9. A (xii) so much so
   B (v) so ... that
10. A (viii) having
    B (iv) once
11. A (vii) therefore
    B (iii) so
12. A (xxv) For example
    B (xxiv) Take ....This

Exercise 6

1. The government plans to help poorer countries by cancelling all third world debt. **Or** ... by the cancellation of ... **Or**: By cancelling/the cancellation of ...
2. Immediately the rules were introduced, congestion was increased/they increased congestion/congestion increased.
3. Government officials have constantly been denying charges of corruption, while secretly accepting bribes from businessmen and lobbyists alike. (**Or** While constantly denying ..., government officials have secretly been accepting ... .)
4. The government plans to boost renewable energy generation will be announced today by Geoff Healey in his first policy move since becoming environment minister.
5. Being a crime against humanity, the destruction of historic buildings for whatever reasons is repellent to many people.
6. Charges for entering city centres will be introduced shortly, raising the cost of motoring.
7. The local authority wants to improve the area by knocking down old tower blocks. **OR**: By knocking ....
8. The project, opposed by both big companies and government departments, aims to regenerate all slum areas in the next decade.
9. The decision marks the beginning of real competition in the electricity market, which was a monopoly for more than a hundred years, until new rules took effect in January, allowing ElectCom to license competition.
10. All car companies are now expected to face stiff competition following a damning report from the EU Competition Commission.
11. The fares have risen substantially over recent years putting people off public transport.
12. Companies need to play on their strengths putting more effort into successful areas, while reducing investment in failing ventures.
13. The government could force through the construction of cheap houses for essential workers by purchasing all the brown-field sites in major cities.
Or: By purchasing all ..., the government could ... **Or**: By the purchase of ..., the government could ...

Exercise 7

1. Mr Forest, president of the company, has upset the vice president and the directors by proposing to sell the firm to one of their rivals in the field, allowing the president to keep his job, but removing the other directors.
2. The drop-in centre offering counselling and supported by the local church is a testament to the government's weakness with the church outdoing it in providing contraception.
3. Mrs Dunn, chairperson on the committee, has alarmed other members with her bid/by bidding to change the constitution of the committee, allowing the chair more powers.
4. The government plans to extend a proposed renewable energy scheme, which will include development of all new hydro projects, may upset environmentalists, who claim that larger projects damage eco-systems and threaten wildlife. *[Note the verb plans in the exercise has been changed to a noun here!]*
5. The government is expected to face stiff opposition to its proposal to ban smoking in all public places for the first time from the autumn, following a report by health experts, damning present government policy.
6. The licences to provide the rail service, which will last 10 years, are intended to help rail companies to secure financial backing by improving punctuality and the standard of service.
7. The government has refused to accept responsibility, while trying to smooth things out behind the scenes.

8. Charges for entering all museums and art galleries will soon be dropped, hopefully leading to an increase in visitor numbers.
9. The report, strongly supported by patients and medics, stated that hospitals should tighten up their appointment procedures.
10. Some people think that pollution will be reduced by recycling materials like bottles and paper.
11. The government plans to boost voting in elections were announced last week by the Home Office Minister immediately after he took up office.

Exercise 8

1. Instead of tackling the result, the underlying cause needs to be addressed.
2. The proposal to legalise cannabis was rushed through resulting in the number of social problems increasing. [**Or**: … resulting in an increase in the number of social problems.]
3. Not having been thought through carefully enough, the venture failed.
4. With more people using it [**Or**: …the system], the system [**Or**: …it] will fall apart soon.
5. The government needs to recruit more police officers to patrol the streets; otherwise, the crime rate will increase.
6. Despite having a number of objections to the introduction of higher taxes on petrol, on balance, I support the policy.
7. Much as I have some objections to the introduction of higher taxes on petrol, on balance, I support the policy.
8. The law having been relaxed, we can focus resources on more serious matters.
9. This is an idea with a number of bad points and a number of good points.
10. Though causing some inconvenience to the public, the idea will be implemented.

Exercise 9

1. as/since/because
2. Planning
3. Having taken/Taking
4. Making/Having made
5. though/as
6. Despite/In spite of/Though
7. If
8. so as not/ in order not
9. otherwise
10. Once/Immediately/After/When

Exercise 10

Unless money is invested in the infrastructure of the country **like** the transport system, a number of problems will arise. **For example,** the system will wear out **and** break down, **causing** serious inconvenience to the travelling public. **This** will have a knock-on effect on the economy in general **with** more people **turning** to cars **and** the roads **becoming** more congested, **which, in turn,** will slow the economy down.

Note that the paragraph contains 68 words.

Exercise 11

Please note that there are other possible ways to connect the text. This is just an example.

Unless public funds in many rich western nations are invested in skills shortages in certain areas, **like** teacher training and teaching, there will be serious repercussions. **First of all/For example,** the educational system will deteriorate further **and** simply collapse, seriously **affecting** the whole of society. **This** will have serious consequences for companies, **which** will turn to other countries where there are no skills shortages to set up new ventures. In my home country**, for example**, factories are being built in areas where there is a surplus of skilled computing staff. **As a result**, governments in more developed countries will have less money from taxes to fund training.

Note that the paragraph contains 107 words.

Exercise 12

1.	J	6.	G	11.	A
2.	E	7.	F	12.	G
3.	C	8.	I	13.	G
4.	C	9.	B	14.	C
5.	D	10.	H		

You might wish to write out the functions for one of the two paragraphs on a piece of paper and then write a paragraph of your own with the functions as your guidelines.

Always remember that functions may be combined in many different ways to form paragraphs. The paragraphs in this exercise are only examples of many different combinations.

Exercise 13

The order of the text is:

◆	11	
◆	1	
◆	10	
◆	12	
◆	5	
◆	7	
◆	8	

◆	2
◆	4
◆	3
◆	6
◆	9
◆	14
◆	13

Exercise 14

1.	A	5.	C	
2.	D	6.	B	
3.	D	7.	B	
4.	A			

Exercise 15

1. g
2. h
3. e
4. a
5. i
6. d
7. f
8. b

As in the previous exercise you may want to use the questions for guidelines when you write.

Exercise 16

1. g
2. d
3. j
4. f
5. c
6. h
7. i
8. a
9. e
10. b

Exercise 17

- 5 c ii
- 7 f iv
- 6 a v
- 2 b vi
- 4 e iii
- 1 g vii
- 3 d i

Exercise 18

The sequence of the first section of the text is: 1 3 5 2 6 [Note text 4 is irrelevant]

The sequence of the second section of the text is: 6 11 10 12 14 [Note texts 7 8 9 13 are irrelevant]

Exercise 19

1. B. This, however,
2. B. Were the government to do this, it D. To do so
3. B. They are both C. Both are
4. A. it B. the findings
5. A. So much so C. It has slowed down so much
6. D. This sensational event
7. B. it
8. B. the increase/ C. the rise – but note the repetition of the word *rose*.
9. A. it B. the venture.
10. C. Having D. Once they had

Exercise 20

1. B. the subject D. it
2. B. There
3. A. These C. These events.
4. C. this improvement
5. A. such a condition
6. C. The ban; D. The restriction
   [This may also be possible.]

7. B. Unfortunately, many of the trees
8. B. To carry out such a proposal
9. B. decriminalisation C. this
10. A. a situation which C. but this

Exercise 21

1. B/L. Not C, because you do not know exactly what *it* refers to; and not F, because of the repetition of *such*.
2. A/C/E/G/K/M/N. F/H/L are almost acceptable, but they involve some repetition, which it is better to avoid. For example, F repeats the word *such*; H is straight out of the first sentence; L is not quite acceptable because the repetition of the word *this* would seem awkward if we use B at 1.
3. A/E/G/J/K/M/N. Note we need to avoid repetition if the item has been used before. Note A/E/G/K/M/N in 2 above.
4. I/P
5. V. Note E and G are perhaps too general here, but N may be acceptable. Again, we must bear in mind the repetition in 2 and 3.
6. Q
7. O
8. U. Note that the word behaviour in this sentence and the grammar rule out the use of F/L here.
9. R
10. T

Exercise 22

The inserted items are marked in bold:

Other **people, however,** are **of the opinion** that wind farms are ugly, **being nothing** more than an eyesore **or** a blot on the landscape. **They point to** the fact that the giant wind turbines, **which** make up the farms are frequently built in remote areas of great beauty. **Moreover, whilst such farms** are inaccessible to most people, **the machines** can be seen from a great distance. **A further downside is** that wind farms may provide safer alternative energy than nuclear power or carbon based energy, **but** they cause greater damage than the pollution **they** are intended to prevent. **The same arguments apply** to windmills at sea, **unless perhaps they** are far enough off the coast not to be seen. **The obvious objections here** are the cost of siting the wind turbines far out to sea and **of bringing the energy back to the shore.**

Exercise 23

1. Example: There are two basic similarities between the two essays. In each essay, the general subject is crime and the essay is organised around focus words: causes and reasons for, which both mean the same thing. The difference is that the first essay title is presented as a question, whereas the second one makes a statement about the present situation as regards crime and then poses a question. In the end, the orgsnisation and the content of the essays are the same.

2. The questions: *How far do you agree? To what extent do you agree?* basically mean the same thing. The main difference here is that the emphasis in A is on *education* and in *B measures such as fines*. You have to be careful with this, especially when you are writing your introduction. You might write: *I agree with the above statement*. For essay title A, this means that you agree that *only education* will help and for B that only measures *such as fines* will help.

3. Essay title A is the same as 2 above The fact that the question asks you to agree or disagree makes no difference If you are asked how far you agree and you answer not at all; then you disagree. The organisation of B here is the same as 3A: How far do you agree? Note, however, that the general subject of the question here has changed. The main subject has changed from fighting an aspect of crime i.e. anti-social behaviour through education to crime in general. It is so easy to misread essay questions and write the wrong answer.

4. Obviously, both essays in A and B are organised around the word *ways* and various synonyms, i.e. *measures, steps etc*. In answering A, you could state that charging people for plastic bags in supermarkets and refunding money on glass bottles is the best way to make people more aware of the damage they cause the environment, but it is easier to say it is one of the ways and describe other measures. This latter option makes the organisation of the question the same as in B. The subject of essay title B is, however, different.

5. The general subject in each essay title here is the same. However, the organisation of each is different. In essay A, the organisation is based around measures/ways etc (How can …?) and benefits. The second essay is asking your opinion about stiffer penalties for abusing animals and what factors are involved in the abuse.

6. The general subjects here are the same, and the focus of each essay is also the same. Both essays are organised around *causes of* and *factors causing* the situation.

7. The general subjects here are the same, The only difference is that the question in A is asking you if you agree (or disagree). You then give your opinion. Title B is telling you that there is a scale to your opinion and asking you where you are: 60% for and 40% against or vice versa.

8. The general subjects of the two essay titles are very different, but the format of the presentation is the same. In both you are given two statements followed by questions directing you to give comments. In essay title A, you are asked to give your opinion and the suggest ways/measures etc. In B, you are asked if anything can be done about the situation presented, i.e. violence…. You can state that something can be done, followed by ways/measures etc. or you can answer the second question and state nothing can be done and say why.

9. The general subjects here are again different and so is the organisation of each. In the first essay, the text is organised around either the arguments for **or** against, not both. Note the word *Discuss* is asking you to describe one or the other. The second essay is similar in that it is asking you to look at one side of the issue in question, i.e. the *disadvantages*.

10. The general subjects are the same, but the organisation in each case is different. Essay title A is asking for your opinion and gives you both sides to choose from. Essay B is organised around the word *problems*.

Exercise 24

1. **Some believe that** the large number of people living in poor accommodation only stores up problems for the future. **They think that** poor housing is a major breeding ground for a vast array of social as well as economic ills. **For example, on the social front,** those living in poor conditions are caught in a cycle of despair **affecting** both their physical and mental health. **This** is, **in turn**, a burden on any country's resources **where** the health and other services have to deal with the situation. **Secondly, on the purely economic front**, poor housing requires continuous costly repairs to the buildings, **which** is a further drain on resources.

2. **In my opinion,** the large number of people living in poor accommodation only stores up problems for the future. **The main reason for this is** poor housing, **which** is a major breeding ground for a vast array of social as well as economic ills. **Take, for example,** those living in poor conditions **who** are caught in a cycle of despair. **The consequent effects on** both their physical and mental health are a burden on any country's resources **where** the health and other services have to deal with the situation. **Similarly**, poor housing requires continuous costly repairs to the buildings, **further** draining resources.

3. **The main cause is** the large number of people living in poor accommodation, **which** only stores up problems for the future, **as** poor housing is a major breeding ground for a vast array of social as well as economic ills. **First,** those living in poor conditions are caught in a cycle of despair, **which** affects both their physical and mental health **and** is **also** a burden on any country's resources. The health and other services **then** have to deal with the situation. **Furthermore,** poor housing requires continuous costly repairs to the buildings - **a** further drain on resources.

4. **My main argument is that** the large number of people living in poor accommodation only stores up problems for the future. Poor housing, **to all intents and purposes**, is a major breeding ground for a vast array of social as well as economic ills. **For example,** those living in poor conditions are caught in a cycle of despair, **which, as a result,** affects both their physical and mental health. **They then become** a burden on any country's resources **with** the health and other services hav**ing** to deal with the situation. **Another problem is that** poor housing requires continuous costly repairs to the buildings, **which further** drains resources.

Exercise 25

Note that at each step in the maze you are making choices. Look at the different ways that the information is presented. At number 1, for example, look at the order of the information: *Travelling is a good example.... a good example to ...is travelling.*

To help you develop the same range and flexibility in writing, cover columns B and C. Now in your head read and try to transform each step of the text into one of the other texts. Now cover columns A and B and do the same and repeat the exercise for column C. A variation of this is to mix the columns. For example, cover texts 1-5 in columns B and C and columns A and B for 6-11.

Key
to
Section 3

Exercise 1

The words in bold below are spelt correctly. The other words are spelt wrongly in the exercise, but they are now correct.

dramatically motivation people **experience environment** government unfortunately **colleague accommodation** separate **plummet** their connection conscientious **discreet difference difficult advantage** disappear **disappointment interested** dispossess **dissolve** dissuade **efficient efficiency embarrassed dictionary** unpleasant **secretary comfortable counsel** programme parliament **interesting psychology simultaneously house television institution** inconvenience **incapable forecast** responsible **machine manufacture** scarce **scenery** vehicle shield

Exercise 2

The words in bold are spelt wrongly. Check the spelling of the other words in the Key for Exercise 1 or in a dictionary.

responsible manufacture **incapible** council programme **eficient mashine coleague** television **instution inconvenence scarse scenry** motivation people experience **enviroment** government unfortunately **conection conscentious unplesant** discrete **diffrence dificult advantige** disappear **dissapointment drammatically** interested dispossess **disolve** dissuade efficiency **embarassed dictionry** secretary **comfortible** plummet their parliament **intresting psichology simultanously** house **forcast** vehicle shield **seperate acommodation**

Note the word **discrete** here and the word **discreet** in Exercise 1. Both spellings are correct, as they are different words.

Exercise 3

The words **in bold** below are correct:

1.   **tomorrow support should** recieve proffesional
2.   **serious salary review receipt** feild **recommend**
3.   pronounciation **photograph permanent particular**
4.   **organise opportunity neighbour necessary** morover
5.   misrable **judgment** interupt interfer **height** [**Judgement** with an **e** is also correct]
6.   **generous foreign favourite familiar** extrordinary
7.   **mention excellent** esential **entertainment** encourag
8.   elswhere sieze therefor **although thorough**
9.   potatoe **whether** wonderfull **yesterday** atmospher
10. **accurate apparatus** chanel **chocolate** ciggarette
11. **circuit** correspondance **equivalent** hereditry **irritate**
12. **February** vegitable chimeney **shoulder** cronology
13. circelation campain succesful stationry **surroundings** [**Stationary and stationery** – what is the difference?]
14. probabilty **priceless prevalent** postpon **pleasure**
15. **phenomenon** plentifull personel persistance percieve

Now that you know that the words which are in ordinary type are wrong, can you correct them? If not, check the spelling of these words in a dictionary.

Exercise 4

The words **in bold** are spelt incorrectly. Can you correct them?

1. Circumstance disease **disguis gaurantee** discriminate
2. **Disperate** hypothesis **themometer** metaphor appropriate
3. **Beleive misellaneous concieve mispelling** beginning
4. **Benifit dangrous** membrane ceremony **droped**
5. Circle **citisen clearence trafic** co-operate **Antartica**
6. **Recomendation commitee** commitment **complementry**
7. **Consceince** science contrary **arguement** cultural
8. **Techniqu** cynical desiccated democracy demographic
9. **Emergenc excesive** prerequisite **featur** ferocious
10. Flight **analisis** gallop gratuitous **genine** great

Exercise 5

1.	television	11.	wonderful
2.	telephone	12.	beautiful
3.	bicycle	13.	familiarise
4.	controversy	14.	family
5.	encourage	15.	information
6.	hazard	16.	guideline
7.	endanger	17.	conscientious
8.	potato	18.	hopeful
9.	endless	19.	advertisement
10.	worthless	20.	education

Exercise 6

1.	incidence	10.	maximum	18.	plunge
2.	consequently	11.	minimum	19.	rocket
3.	environment	12.	decline	20.	trough
4.	government	13.	plummet	21.	economic
5.	intervene	14.	trend	22.	cinema
6.	introduce	15.	contrast	23.	particularly
7.	largely	16.	product	24.	programme
8.	illiterate	17.	forecast	25.	business
9.	magnificent				

When you find words that you have difficulty remembering how to spell, you could keep a list of them without the vowels as in this exercise and the previous one. For example, the word *receive*, you could add in your list and then write the full word opposite:

r _ c _ _ v_. ————————→ receive

Then you can test yourself for your own particular mistakes!!

Exercise 7

1. sea/tea/pea
2. idea
3. main/pain/rain/vain/fail/sail etc
4. banana
5. house/mouse
6. eight
7. weight/height
8. their
9. receive
10. believe
11. available
12. various
13. variety
14. interest
15. enough
16. shield/friend
17. measure
18. feeling
19. repetition/television
20. telephone
21. economic

Exercise 8

1. employee
2. sentence
3. dictionary
4. possibility
5. strength
6. potato/tomato
7. library
8. language
9. policeman
10. policewoman
11. psychology
12. exhausted
13. environment
14. bicycle
15. dangerous
16. pollution
17. confused
18. congested
19. holiday
20. thought/brought
21. ought
22. daughter
23. exercise
24. politician
25. permission
26. people
27. February
28. secretary
29. computer
30. conscious

Exercise 9

The words in bold were spelt incorrectly in the exercise.

1. The accommodation available to people in lower income groups is usually very **inadequate**.
2. A completely new suite of rooms is **essential** to house the new equipment.
3. Frequently the **planning** is not particularly thorough, so that when it comes to carrying out any work, there are **invariably** delays.
4. There are not **enough** teachers to provide adequate cover in schools.
5. **Inventions** in the world of technology are now **practically** a **daily occurrence**.
6. It is hardly **acceptable** to expect private **businesses** to shoulder the whole f**inancial burden**.
7. The remedy applied by most **governments** has been to introduce swingeing cuts to **their** manpower only to rehire them again at greater cost, once they realise that they have lost **personnel** with invaluable experience.
8. **Gauging** the mood of the electorate requires considerable political skill.
9. Everyone has **benefited** from the advances in the medical **field** that we have **witnessed** in recent years.
10. News **bulletins** are now **transmitted** round the clock, almost **overwhelming** us with up-to-date information.

11. The number of young people entering higher education from poor backgrounds is a **shining** example of what can be **achieved.**
12. Once the idea has been **thought through carefully**, it will not be long **before** everyone is taking it up **wholeheartedly.**
13. **Professionalism** in most fields of work is now in such short **supply** that the best one can hope for is **mediocrity.**
14. **Appropriate** measures should be taken to **ensure** that rioting does not take place at any sporting event.
15. Some people argue that so many old traditions have been **superseded** by modern or **foreign** ideas that we are in danger of **losing** our national identity.
16. **Attention** should now be focused on **equipping** as many tertiary level students as possible with laptops.

Note the word *swingeing* in number 7.

Note that in number 16 you can have *focused* or *focussed.*

Exercise 10

The unjumbled words are in bold.

We **associate** being rich with not having a care in the **world**, with **comfort** and feeling safe and secure. **Wealth** is seen as the **answer** to the many problems in life.

Having huge **amounts** of money at one's **disposal** is, ironically, a **difficult** problem to deal with. People are **steeped** in the **belief** that being rich represents security. But does it? To protect accumulated **possessions**, no matter how small the amount, seemingly countless **measures** are needed by the rich, and not so rich, to protect **their** property. The burglar **alarms** and security bars on windows and doors of today, however, will seem **primitive** to the security of the future. The very well-off already living in fortified compounds will have **access** to hand/iris recognition devices to enter their property. Yet, every solution tends to bring about another scenario to be **dealt** with. So, what if the hand is cut off or the eye removed? The answer is make sure the device can only **recognise** live irises and hands. Problem solved. No, not exactly. You can be **kidnapped**. That's where the body-guards come in. But can you trust them? Perhaps, **there** is only one way out: if something is **causing** you a problem, the sensible thing to do is to get rid of it!

Exercise 11

The missing words are in bold.

Most, if not all, people have certain things that **they** think **are** impossible to do. Take dealing **with** domestic chores. For some of us, summoning enough energy to tidy **our** rooms or flats or sort out months of paper or to change the bed all require a lot of effort. At work, also, tackling even **the** simplest tasks sometimes seems **as** insurmountable as more complex jobs.

So it **is** not exactly surprising that for many people stepping outside the limits of their experience or beliefs **is** almost out of the question. It **is** difficult to change people's habits and views of **the** world. Yet, fortunately, there have been, and still are, individuals **who** have influenced mankind, because they challenged tradition. Few of us dare to hold **an** opinion **that** has no currency within the teachings we have learnt. **Being** original among our peers and family also sets us apart **and** we then become targets of jealousy or envy. To develop **an** outlook that is broader than one's friends or that is just different is dangerous, but it is something, which must **be** encouraged if we are to develop. Wilde said that we **are** all in the gutter, but some of us are gazing at the stars. In **the** modern era, will the star-gazers prevail?

Exercise 12

It *[is]* good to make mistakes **in spite** of what some people might think. Many of us go through our lives in sheer **terror** of doing something wrong, **because** we have *[been]* taught that every task should always be performed correctly. This is **nonsense**, however. This is obviously where teaching children comes in.

A good part of the problem, I feel, lies not with the mistakes themselves, but with **labelling** aspects of the learning process as errors rather *[than]* seeing them as a natural, and **necessary**, **development**. Doing things in the wrong way should surely be avoided. Take children as an example. They have to fall down in order to learn to stand *[up]* again; the same **applies** to everything that they do, including mental tasks. If children at school or at home *[are]* constantly **harassed** about doing everything correctly, there is a good chance they will just give up. It is possible for them then to become afraid of **opening** themselves up to the censure of others. Yet, children need surely to make mistakes in order to see what is right and not to be constantly snapped at for failure.

Adults **learning** to use new technology are also a case in point. Computers are able to check for spelling mistakes, which is a helpful tool. And what about learning to drive, which is also fun? Grown-ups may have **difficulties** mastering the process and make lots of mistakes, but those who concentrate on their failures rather than **acquiring** the skill they are trying to learn tend to give up. By contrast, those who *[are]* focused on the task rather than their mistakes usually **succeed**.

And the solution? The simple answer is to **train** people to treat mistakes and **minor** hiccups as natural steps in the process of learning. Teachers and trainers could point *[out]* that, although students should aim to be perfect, they must realise that they are going to make mistakes and learn from them. This positive **attitude** will help build confidence and stop people giving up. On a general note, if people are constantly making mistakes, new discoveries will not be made.

Note that in English spelling labelling is spelt with double 'l' and in American a single 'l'.
Note that in the fourth sentence of the second paragraph it is probably more precise to write *stand up* than just *stand*.

You can see from this exercise that it is difficult to look for different mistakes at the same time. While you are practising for the exam, look for each type of mistake separately and then gradually try to look for all the mistakes simultaneously.

It is difficult sometimes to see spelling mistakes in a longer text as the mind is concentrating on various things at the same time. One technique is to scan the line backwards checking the word for spelling rather than reading it. You can also do this in a zigzag up and down the paragraph from left to right or right to left. With these methods you may not find all of the mistakes; see the word leaning/learning above. Here you have to stop and look at the context.

Exercise 13

It is good to make mistakes in spite of what some people **[should: might]** think. Many of us go through our lives in sheer terror of doing something wrong, because we have been taught that every task should always be performed correctly. This is nonsense, however.

A good part of the problem, I feel, lies not with the mistakes themselves, but with labelling **the** aspects of the learning process as errors rather than seeing them as a natural, and necessary, development. Take **the** children as an example. They have to fall down in order to learn to stand up again; the same applies to everything that they do, including mental tasks. If children at **the** school or at home are constantly harassed about doing everything correctly, there is a good chance they will just give up. It is possible for them then to become afraid of opening themselves up to the censure of others. Yet, **the** children need surely to make mistakes in order to see what is right and not to be constantly snapped at for failure.

Adults learning to use **the** new technology are also a case in point. Computers are able to check for spelling mistakes, which is a helpful tool. They **[must: may]** have difficulties mastering the process and make lots of **the** mistakes, but those who concentrate on their failures rather than acquiring the skill they are trying to learn tend to give up. By contrast, those who are focused on the task rather than their mistakes tend to succeed.

And the solution? The simple answer is to train **the** people to treat mistakes and **the** minor hiccups as natural steps in the process of learning. **The** teachers and trainers could point out that, although students should aim to be perfect, they must realise that they are going to make mistakes and learn from them. This positive attitude will help build **the** confidence and stop people giving up.

Exercise 14

The corrected prepositions are in bold.

1. While I have considerable sympathy **with** this idea, there are certain aspects that I do not approve **of**.
2. **In** 2000, people were filled with new optimism.
3. It is not really sensible to rely on data, no matter where they come from.
4. There has been considerable improvement **in** the way business is conducted over the past few years.
5. The success **of** any venture depends **on** a host of variables.
6. The money should not be spent **on** weapons but **on** education, the infrastructure, etc.
7. Our attitude to work needs to change; otherwise, more jobs will be lost.
8. While this may be an advantage to some, a considerable number of people will see little benefit **from** it.
9. No country should interfere **with/in** the affairs of another nation.
10. Few people believe that the legalisation of soft drugs is an improvement on the current situation.
11. People's views **on** the subject are difficult to gauge.
12. Some people argue that there is no point **in** the government putting more money into public services unless efficiency is increased.
13. Although I object to some aspects of this argument, my views **on** this matter generally do not differ from the writer's.
14. Many qualified teachers are still lacking **in** basic skills and training.
15. It is well known that teenagers have enormous influence over each other.
16. There is a serious lack **of** qualified teachers in this field.
17. This is, however, dependent on certain criteria being fulfilled.
18. People in general do not think carefully enough **about** the consequences of their actions.
19. Some people, by contrast, are struggling daily **to find** basic needs in order to survive.
20. I largely agree **with** you **on** the above matter.
21. The government has succeeded **in alienating** the electorate very quickly.
22. The city council needs to think **about** this matter more carefully before it proceeds **with** the pedestrianisation of the centre.
23. The key to this problem is not as obvious as it first appears.

Exercise 15

The corrections are in brackets [ ] and in bold.

1. During October, visitor[ ] numbers fell off their [S]eptember [peak], [dropping] over 40,000 visitors by the end of the year. [Note the second verb in the –ing form.]
2. The data show[ ] that the trend was [obviously] upwards. [Note that the word data is plural!]
3. Picking up [in] 1999, [numbers] leapt considerably. [Note the two verbs have the same subject. If the –ing form of the verb is first, the subject relating to both goes with the main verb.]
4. The improvement in [the] year 2001 was marked by [sales surging or a sales surge] to 5 million[ ] euros.
5. [The] number of people [visiting] the museum [rose] [approximately] 30,000 a month [throughout] the year 2000.
6. The rise [in visitor numbers] in July was gradual.
7. In 2001, 20 million[ ] copies of the book were sold.
8. The steady increase in attendances from 30,000 to around 45,000 in the first four month[s] [was] followed by a sharper rise in May.
9. In the year 1990, sales shot [up] significantly.
10. The map show[s] the changes [that] took place in the area [spanning] a [period] of 25 years.
11. The airport [was] considerably enlarged by the [purchase] of two [areas] of land.
12. In 1986, an [extension] was buil[t] to the house.
13. [The table shows] the [percentage] of women in [government] posts in [the] years 1960 to 2000.
14. [T]he trend was fairly [erratic], with a 2% drop to 13% in 1965,[ ] followed by a [rise] of 1% five year[s] [later]. [Note the word *was* is not needed here. The second verb is a past participle.]
15. By contrast, sales increased to 13%, [doubling] to 26 per cent by 1975.

Exercise 16

The corrections are in brackets [ ] and in bold.

1. The bar chart show[s] the [projected/estimated/anticipated etc] profits in thousands of dollars.
2. Growth [is] expected to slow [until] 2004, after which it [is] estimated that [it] will even [out.]
3. By contrast, it is forecasted that the sales of computer games will [outstrip] music CDs in the [near or put no adjective] future. [Note you can write forecasted or forecast.]
4. DIY sales will rise [fitfully], [increasing/climbing etc to avoid repetition] at [the] rate of 10 percent per month.
5. Sales are projected to [stay/remain] steady for the [remaining/next] three years. [Choose one or the other to avoid repetition].
6. Wyers Ltd is expected to make a [loss] of 2 million euro[s] in [its] first year of trading[.]
7. According to the chart, from 2007 until 2009 inclusive, the town [is] expected to experience negative population growth.
8. The population will fall [ ] gradually over the next five years from 2010 to 2015.
9. The [number of people] will grow [ ] [by] 20%.
10. As far as hotel [occupancy] rates [are concerned], it is expected that over the period they will [exceed] all expectations.
11. Falling [initially] by 10% in the last quarter of the year, growth in sales will pick [up] next year.
12. Thereafter, however, the [population] growth in London [is] anticipated to be much slower.
13. After that sales went up and down wildly, first doubling to 400 units, and subsequently falling again to the [March] level. [These] fluctuations [were] followed by [relative] stability.
14. From this level, the number of motorcycles sold [jumped] dramatically, [hitting] a peak of just under 100.
15. This was followed by a sharp drop of about 80 % in the number of [videos purchased].

Exercise 17

The verbs which are in bold, are in the correct place below.

Some people **believe** that **using** comics to **encourage** children **to read** more **is** not a good way **to tackle** the problem of illiteracy. They **think** that the pictures **discourage** readers from **thinking** for themselves and so **using** comics **is** another step in the **dumbing** down of the educational process. However, nothing **could be** further from the truth. Anything, comics included, which **induces** children, or indeed adults, **to read should be encouraged**. For my own part, I **was introduced** to some of the classic tales through picture books **telling** stories as indeed **were** many of my friends. **Take** the example of films **based** on books. When such films **are released** the sales of the books invariably **soar**. The same **applies** to books **made** into TV series. With comics, it **is** really no different. They **are** just one step away from **reading** a book. ...

Exercise 18

1. **Sport has a wide range of benefits.** 2. First, at an international level, **it** encourages people from different cultures to come into contact with each other, **3. which** then helps to break down barriers between different countries, **4. and** furthers international cooperation. **5. Take [for example,/for instance]** amateur sports meetings between schools and universities in different parts of the world **[, for example/,for instance]. 6.** Many countries arrange contacts **like this/of this kind 7. so that** people at different levels in their respective societies develop closer bonds, **8. such as/like** cultural exchanges or trade links. **9. This** is obviously of mutual benefit to all concerned.

10. While some people are reluctant to take up any kind of sporting activity, **11. there is** overwhelming evidence that playing sport can have a very positive effect on health. **12. Physical/All physical activity** improves coordination and, **at the same time/also** increases well-being, 13. **as it [Or in fact, it]** helps fight against disease, **14. thus enhancing** the quality of people's lives.

Notes

2.   The word *football* is too specific here. You need a word that simply refers back to the word *Sport*.
3.   The word *which* cannot begin a sentence like this. Note the change in punctuation after the word *other*.
4.   Both parts of the sentence are equal. There is no contrast.
5.   Note that this part of the text is an example. It cannot stand as it is without a verb. You can add the word *take* on its own or you can add the adverbs as shown in bold.
6.   You need some kind of connection between this sentence and the previous one. Can you think of any others?
7.   Note that the text in 7 is a purpose, not a reason. Note that there is no comma after the word *kind*.
8.   These are examples, not a finite list.
9.   The word *It* is confusing here. What can it refer to?
10. And 11. Note that *While* is a conjunction, which means that the texts in 10 and 11 form one sentence without the word *however*. This is a common mistake.
12. The word *Activity* on its own is too general. You need to relate the sentence to the context, somehow. *On the other hand* is obviously not suitable, as there is no contrast.
13. This part of the text can be a reason. If you look at the original text in Section 2 Exercise 12 you will see it is presented as an explanation. Both are acceptable.
14. This is a result.

Exercise 19

The text with the punctuation in the correct place is as follows:

Admittedly, employers do have the right to make sure that the people who work for them are not using their work time for their own purposes. Whilst it is impossible to deny the truth of this opinion, I personally feel that the invasion of an individual's privacy, by allowing employers to check on employees' e-mails and electronic work, is unacceptable. Employers can now track every piece of work done. For example, they can check everything workers do on their computers: what work they have done; what games they have played; what they have looked at on the internet. They can also check whether the e-mails are related to their work or whether they are private. Surely, all of this amounts to an invasion of the individual's privacy.

Exercise 20

1.   There **are**, however, several reasons why the situation **needs** to be dealt with as a soon as possible.
2.   Many people evidently agree with this point of **view/ these points of view**.
3.   These new toys, which come on the market at regular intervals, **put** enormous pressure on **parents** with young **children**.
4.   Few are able to understand the complexity of this concept, but it **does** not mean that it should be ignored.
5.   Beautiful surroundings are important for people's sense of well-being.
6.   The computer, whether in the field of **work** or in the home, **is** the source of as much good as **it is** of harm.
7.   Being in beautiful surroundings **is** important for one's sense of well-being.
8.   Self-awareness **does** not as a rule come easily to everyone.
9.   As far as safety and comfort on public transport **are** concerned, there is surely no room for equivocation on the part of the powers that be.
10.   More attention than necessary **has** been devoted to this issue already.
11.   In recent **years**, people have been more willing to accept greater stress at work than previously.
12.   The future of the car industry is certainly secure, because people will always want to travel by private transport rather than a public system which **is** at the mercy of lack of funding and poor management.
13.   At first glance, it would appear that all the available avenues **have** been exhausted, but there **is** a raft of measures that can be implemented.
14.   The growth of e-mail and the increasing flexibility of employers **mean** many people are turning to tele-working.
15.   More than one in four of the workforce now works from home.
16.   About two thirds of the workforce in this field are **women**.
17.   We must ask **ourselves** whether it is acceptable for money to be poured into the arts when so many people are living below the poverty **line**.
18.   European painters such as Leonardo da Vinci, Raphael, Van Gogh etc **are** often more widely known than more contemporary **artists**.
19.   The use of mobile phones **is** spreading rapidly among young people.
20. **Politicians** need to put greater effort into sorting out the mess in the education world.
21.   Another problem here **is** the cost to the poor, once the measure **has** been introduced.
22.   **Information** like advice depends largely on the experience of those that one obtains **it** from.
23.   The government are now in a quandary over this situation. [Note in British English government can be singular or plural.]
24.   There **is** little to choose between the two answers.

Key
to
Section 4

The Key in this Section contains a selection of model answers, 21 in total, with *possible* band scores. Note that the Key does not contain answers for all the tests. However, in some cases, there are several versions of an answer, with different scores.

The possible band scores are mostly in the 6 - 9 range with one example of a band 5. All of the texts with the exception of the Band 5 are free of mistakes. Obviously, if any of the texts contained mistakes, this would affect the score.

Test 1 Task 1 Version 1

The bar chart shows the results of a survey of young professionals aged 20-30, who were asked to state which factors they thought gave them an incentive to succeed.

The factors divide into three main groups. These are personal (both positive and negative) and external, and the personal group is the larger. In the first group, *Personal satisfaction* and *Ambition* are mentioned by 80% of the people who were asked and 50% of people give *Desire for material things* and 45% give *Money*. Of the more negative personal things, *Rivalry* is mentioned by 50% of the people in the sample as a factor that motivates them to succeed. Other factors that are in this second sub-group are *Feeling inadequate, Envy/Jealousy* and *Fear of failure,* which are given as 34%, 30% and 25%.

Turning now to the external factors, the highest amount goes to *Family pressure,* which is stated by 70% of the poll sample, followed by *Pressure from society* at 60% and *Peer pressure* at 45%.

It is clear that success among young preffessionals depends mainly on self-motivating factors.

Word Count: 179 words

Possible Band: 7

Test 1 Task 1 Version 2

The bar chart shows the results of a survey of young professionals aged 20-30, who were asked to state which factors they thought gave them an incentive to succeed.

The factors divide into three main groups, namely: personal (both positive and negative) and external, with the former being the larger of the two. In the first group, *Personal satisfaction* and *Ambition* are mentioned by 80% of those surveyed with *Desire for material things* and *Money* being given by 50% and 45%, respectively. Of the more negative personal factors, *Rivalry* is cited by 50% of respondents as being a factor motivating them to succeed. Other factors that make up this latter sub-group are *Feeling inadequate, Envy/Jealousy* and *Fear of failure* at 34%, 30% and 25% respectively.

Among the external factors, the highest rating goes to *Family pressure*, which is quoted by 70% of the poll sample, followed by *Pressure from society* at 60% and *Peer pressure* at 45%.

It is clear that success among young preffessionals depends mainly on self-motivating factors.

Word Count: 170 words

Possible Band: 8

Test 1 Task 2 Version 1

The so-called 'brain drain' from poor to rich countries is now robbing poorer countries of essential workers like doctors, nurses, engineers, and the trend will continue, if not to get worse.

Some people say this movement of people around the world is not new. People have always been attracted by the wider choice of employment and greater opportunity in big cities in their own countries and abroad. As the technological age advances, richer countries do not have enough workers to keep up with the development. So they turn to other parts of the world to find the workers they need. Many richer European countries, for example, are now trying to attract skilled IT workers from my home country India by offering higher salaries than they could get at home. With globalisation, many people feel that the process cannot be stopped.

Others like myself think that measures should be taken to improve the situation. For example, rich countries could compensate poorer countries for the loss of investment in the people they have trained, like doctors, nurses, teachers and dentists. However, this may be difficult to organise, but an attempt could be made to get it started. Another step, which has already begun to happen, is to use the forces of globalisation itself. Western countries could encourage people to stay in their own countries by direct investment in projects like computer factories. Or they could send more patients abroad for treatment, as is already happening.

It is obviously difficult to stop the movement around the world and it is probably foolish to try to stop it, but attempts should be made to improve the situation.

Word Count: 273 words

Possible Band: 7

Test 1 Task 2 Version 2

The so-called 'brain drain' from poor to rich countries is now robbing poorer countries of essential personnel like doctors, nurses, engineers, and the trend is set to continue, if not to get worse.

Some people say this movement of people around the world is not a new phenomenon. Migrant workers have always been attracted by the wider choice of employment and greater opportunity in major cities in their own countries and abroad. Recently, as the technological age has advanced and as richer countries find themselves with not enough workers to feed their development, they have had to turn to other parts of the world to find the necessary manpower. Many richer European countries, for example are now trying to attract skilled IT workers from my home country India by offering higher salaries than they could hope to earn at home. With the globalisation of the world economy, many people feel that the process cannot be stopped.

Others, myself included, are of the opinion that measures should be taken to address the problem, by compensating poorer countries financially for the loss of investment in the people they have trained, like doctors and nurses. Admittedly, this may be cumbersome to administer, but an attempt could be made to get it off the ground. Another step, which in part has already begun to happen, is to use the forces of globalisation itself. Western countries could encourage people to stay in their own countries by direct investment in projects like computer factories or by sending patients abroad for treatment, as is already happening.

It is obviously difficult to restrict the movement of people around the world and it is probably foolish to try to stop it, but attempts should be made to redress the imbalance.

Word Count: 291 words

Possible Band: 9

Test 2 Task 1 Version 1

The chart shows the results of a survey of theatre-goers about what annoys them most during a theatre performance.

As can be seen from the diagram, there are two main groups of irritants: those which are related to noise and non-noise irritants, and of the two the second is the larger. *Rustling sweet papers* is the most irritating action for 90% of those in the sample, and *Coughing* is the next at 75%. *Whispering* comes next at 60% and *Sneezing* at 45%. In this group, *Snoring* is mentioned as annoying to 30% of those in the sample. *Mobile phones* annoy 50% of the people and *Bleeps* 40%.

As for non-noise irritants, *Arriving late* at 70% is the main one. The next highest in this category is *Tall people* who disturb 30% of those in the sample and *Big hairdos* next at 23%. *Flash photography* disturbs 25% of theatre-goers, but the lowest in this group is *Armrest hogging* at 20%.

Word count: 159

Possible Band: 7

Test 2 Task 1 Version 2

The chart shows the results of a survey of theatre-goers as to what annoys them most during a theatre performance.

As we can see from the diagram, there is a number of irritants for theatre-goers. *Rustling sweet papers* is the most irritating action for 90% of the people who were part of the survey of theatre-goers and *Coughing* is the next highest at 75%. *Whispering* comes next at 60% and then *Sneezing at* 45%. Of this group, *Snoring* is annoying to 30% of the theatre-goers. *Mobile phones* annoy 50% of people and *Bleeps* annoy 40%. These are all about noise.

There are also some irritants in the survey of theatre-goers that are not about noise. *Arriving late* at 70% is the main one. The next highest in this group is *Tall people* who disturb 30% of the theatre-goers and *Big hairdos* is next at 23%. *Flash photography* irritates 25% of people, but the lowest in this group is *Armrest hogging* at 20%.

Word count: 162

Possible Band: 6

Test 2 Task 2

The criticism that alternative energy sources such as wind power etc. cause as much environmental damage as fossil fuel has some justification Some people, for example, are strongly against the use of wind power. Indeed, the large wind farms in some European countries have come in for strong criticism and not just from environmentalists. They are very ugly, even if they are in the sea far away from the coast. Burning household waste for fuel also causes problems, because of the harmful fumes that are the by-product of the process. So while the amount of waste put into landfill sites is reduced thus preserving the environment, the air is being polluted instead! However, in my opinion, such sources need to be encouraged as a means of replacing fossil fuel as they have considerable advantages.

First of all, as the technology for using alternative sources of energy is becoming more and more sophisticated, any harmful by-product will be minimised. Moreover, the cost of producing the necessary equipment will decline. Take solar energy, for example. In the past, the panels that were needed to utilise energy from the sun were huge and not very environmentally friendly. Now, however, the same panels are small enough not to be noticed or are made to look like say roof tiles or normal parts of vehicles. The same will apply to wind farms as the giant turbines become smaller and less obvious.

Energy from water also comes in for a lot of criticism. This has come about from the many high profile dam projects around the world where huge areas have been destroyed both for people and local flora and fauna. However, it is a safer alternative to nuclear energy and a price that has to be paid.

Whilst any form of energy that we seek to utilise is going to cause some damage, I feel that wind, sun and water have to be harnessed for the good of the environment.

Word count: 325

Possible Band: 8

Test 3 Task 1 Version 1

The chart shows the value in dollars of three companies selling farming equipment every five years from 1960 until 2000 and their projected value up to 2012.

Greenacres Ltd increased its value by more than double between 1960 and the year 1990. The value rose from 2 million dollars to over 4 million dollars. The value dropped by about 25% by 1995 and then by another million by the year 2000. Then it was valued at 2 million dollars. The trend for Carsons Limited was steady and upwards with fluctuations and it doubled its value from 500,000 dollars to one million dollars by 2000. Farm Implements Ltd, existed for the first time in 1980. However, by the year 2000, its value was about 2 million dollars, which was up from its value of 1 million dollars in 1980. Farm Implements Ltd, will increase in value gradually until 2012.

Greenacres Ltd and Carsons Ltd will both increase in value until 2012 and Greenacres Ltd will recover to the peak of just above 4 million dollars in 1990. And Carsons Ltd is expected to continue its increase to a value of 1.5 million dollars by 2012.

Word count: 194

Possible Band: 6

Test 3 Task 1 Version 2

The chart shows the value in dollars of three companies selling farming equipment every five years from 1960 until 2000 and their projected value up to 2012.

Whilst Greenacres Ltd more than doubled in value between 1960 and the year 1990, rising from 2 million dollars to just over 4 million, the value dropped by approximately 25% by 1995 and then by another third by the year 2000, when it was valued at 2 million dollars. In contrast, the trend for Carsons Limited was steadily upwards with some fluctuations and a doubling in value from 500,000 dollars to one million by the year 2000. The third company, Farm Implements Ltd, was not set up until 1980. However, by the year 2000, its value stood at approximately 2 million dollars, doubling from its 1980 value of 1 million. Farm Implements Ltd, is expected to increase in value gradually until 2012.

Until 2012, Greenacres Ltd and Carsons Ltd are both expected to increase in value with the former recovering to match the peak of just above 4 million dollars last seen in 1990. Similarly, Carsons Ltd is set to continue its steady increase reaching a value of 1.5 million dollars by 2012.

Word count: 200

Possible Band: 8

Test 3 Task 2

The debate about how to assess students at university has been raging as long as such institutions have existed. In one group are those who believe that the only sure way to test the ability to study or achievement is through formal examinations.

The increased use of the internet has shown the difficulty that teachers have in assessing their students' course work. Students can download vast amounts of material from the web. In fact, it is impossible for a teacher to know whether the student did, in fact, do the work himself. The student may have done part of the work for a project, but it is difficult for the tutor to assess the student properly. The problem then is that if the teacher ignores the possibility that the student stole the ideas from somewhere else, a body of workers will be produced who are not really up to the job.

In the other group, are those who feel that formal written exams are wrong and that assessment should be continuous throughout a course. There are students who do not perform well under pressure in exams. They may know the information that they are asked to write about very well, but may not be able to perform. So it would be wrong to destroy someone's career just because of this. Furthermore, the numbers here are not insignificant, so the effect on the job market would be high.

The answer, I feel, lies somewhere in the middle. A university degree should be based on a combination of both forms of assessment. The proportion of marks given to each type of assessment could depend on the nature of the course. For example, a particular course, say an MA, may be more research based work, which would be better assessed by course work like essays etc. In this case however, it is still wise to have an examination like an oral or a viva where the student is examined in detail about the content of what they have written.

Word count: 336 words

Possible Band: 7

Test 4 Task 1

The table shows the percentage of pupils who secured places at higher educational establishments from 1995 to 1996 inclusive.

Of the five schools, Harble Secondary made the most significant improvement, with the percentage of higher education entrants increasing from 30 to 80 students by the end of the period. Greystone High, on the other hand, which sent three times the number of entrants on to higher education as Harble Secondary in 1991, experienced a significant drop in percentage terms to 40 in 2001.

The other three secondary schools followed similar patterns with numbers from Fairfield Girls on the rise from 65 to 79 and Royston Academy climbing from 50 to 60 places secured.

Crackend Boys was the only school where the number of entrants to higher education remained approximately at the same level throughout the period, ending up just two percent in 1995.

Generally speaking, four out of the five secondary schools increased the number of pupils they sent on to higher education over the period.

Word count: 166 words

Possible Band: 7 [Note that the data in the description is factually incorrect. If the data were corrected, it would be a possible Band 9. Does the table give numbers or percentages?]

Test 4 Task 2

Travelling like everything has two sides. For some people, it only serves to confirm their prejudices, whereas for others it acts as a means of education and broadens the mind.

First of all, visiting other countries abroad can help people of all ages learn languages, so that they broaden their experiences. For example, learning a language in the country in which it is spoken is very different from studying it in one's home country. For myself, coming to this country has enabled me to improve my English and meet new friends. Similarly, while moving around a country, travellers can learn about the geography and local culture rather than relying on books or other media as sources of information. For my own part, having first hand knowledge of the United Kingdom has been invaluable. I understand the culture more and can make decisions for myself rather than have them made for me by other people.

Unfortunately, there is a downside to travelling. People frequently feel nervous when they travel, either through excitement or through anxiety about what is to come. In such circumstances people tend to be more critical of the treatment they receive. How often has one heard: where I come from it isn't done like this or we do it this way? It is hardly surprising that this happens when the same thing occurs with people visiting others in different parts of their own country. Think what happens when people get married!

Travelling will continue to enrich the minds of some, but, unfortunately, it will confirm the prejudices of others. This is human nature.

Word count: 265 words

Possible Band: 7

Test 5 Task 1

The diagram shows the results of a survey carried out on a sample of 1,000 people on the different sources of noise, which are a nuisance.

The information may be divided into four categories according to their degree of annoyance. There is nothing in the *Not annoying* category. Four sources of noise fall within the largest category, *Extremely annoying*. Of these, the noise source which people found the most irritating was *Barking dogs*, followed closely by *DIY* and then *Mobile phones*. The least annoying cause of noise in this group was *Music*.

Moving on to the second category, *Very annoying*, it contains two items: *Radios* and *Aeroplanes* with the first causing more of a disturbance than the second.

In the third category, *Annoying*, it can be seen that *TVs* cause more of a nuisance than *Radios*. As for *Pianos*, they were considered as only being *Fairly annoying* by those in the sample.

It is clear that *Barking dogs* is the most annoying noise source.

Word Count: 164

Possible Band: 7

Test 5 Task 2

Throughout the world, the populations of the major cities are increasing at a fast rate and where land for building is not available, there is enormous pressure to build upwards rather than sideways.

The main advantage of building higher buildings is that they can take the pressure off the need to build just outside large cities, thus preventing the spread outwards and the destruction of the countryside. In smaller countries, land is very expensive and so it makes sense to build upwards. In London, for example, property prices are rising rapidly and will continue to do so for years to come unless more homes are built. Both options, building in the greenbelt around the city and constructing skyscapers are controversial, but tall buildings are the less damaging alternative.

Another benefit is more accommodation and workspace inside cities, as it shortens the distance that people have to travel to work. Stress is reduced by this and people feel healthier. Moreover, as it is possible to provide more accommodation in a smaller ground space by building upwards, the cost of living is cheaper.

However, some people are against the idea of building skyscapers to solve the lack of space problem. High blocks of flats in the past have been the source of a lot of social ills. People feel cut off from the environment and feel better if they have a garden, however small. People also object to tall buildings, because they feel trapped in them and they worry about escaping if something goes wrong. Although I understand the reservations that people have, I feel that it is better to preserve the countryside and build upwards rather than sideways.

Word Count: 277

Possible Band: 7

Test 5 Task 2 Version 2

Nowadays the populations of the major cities are growing fast. Where there is no land for building, there is big pressure to \build up and not sideways.

The first benefit of building higher buildings is that they reduce the need to build outside big cities. This stops the spread outwards and stops the destruction of the countryside. In smaller countries, land is very expensive. It makes sense to build upwards. In London, for example, property prices are rising rapidly and will continue. More homes need to be built. Building in the greenbelt around the city and building high buildings is controversial, but the tall buildings are less damaging.

Another benefit is more accommodation and workspace inside cities. It shortens the distance that people have to travel to work. Stress is reduced by this and people feel healthier. Moreover, it is possible to provide more accommodation in a smaller ground space with tall buildings and so the cost of living is cheaper.

But some people are against building skyscapers to solve the lack of space problem. High blocks of flats in the past were the source of a lot of social problems. People feel separate from the environment and feel better if they have a garden, even if it is small. People also do not like tall buildings, because they feel trapped in them. They also worry about escaping if something goes wrong. I understand why people do not like tall buildings, but I feel that it is better to keep the countryside and build upwards.

Word Count: 255

Possible Band: 6

Test 6 Task 1 Version 1

The maps show the changes in the size and in the value of the land per hectare of West Farm over a period of 90 years from 1900 to 1990.

In 1900, the area covered by West Farm was 5,000 hectares and the value of one hectare was one dollar. By the year 1925, while the size of the farm was 850 hectares, the value of the land had leapt to 20 dollars a hectare, which gave a total of 17,000 dollars. Fifteen years later, however, the farm had increased in size to 1,700 hectares, but the value of a hectare had only increased by 25% to 25 dollars. The property was, nevertheless valued at 42,500 dollars.

In 1970, while West Farm with only 500 hectares was much smaller than it had been in the previous 70 years, the value of the property was higher than ever before at 50,000 dollars.

The size of West Farm had jumped to 3,500 hectares by 1990 with the value per hectare climbing by 25% to 125 dollars, totalling 437,500 dollars.

It is clear that the value of West Farm increased significantly over the period.

Word Count: 191 words.

Possible Band: 7

Test 6 Task 2

Nowadays woods and forests in all countries in the world are losing trees as more land is needed for building and farming and more wood is needed for the construction industry, for fuel and for paper. However, we need trees and plants to provide us with the oxygen we breathe. So the destruction of trees is a threat to our survival.

The matter is not just in the hands of governments and big companies. The solution to the problem is one of partnership between governments and big companies and ordinary individuals. Take newspapers, for example. Newspapers are made from paper which comes from wood pulp. However, there is little need for them to be made totally from wood pulp. In fact, in many cases, papers are now made from over 60% recycled paper. This has come about through pressure from the government to encourage recycling and from the environmentalists made up of individuals. Stricter controls could be placed on companies to ensure that the remaining 40 percent comes from more recycled paper and from forests that are renewed. However, the final responsibility here is on individuals to put pressure on the governments and big companies and in the end to collect paper for recycling.

A very simple measure is for individuals, groups like schools and companies to sponsor the planting of new trees. When a lot of people come together in this way, it can be very effective. Trees could be planted in schools and children could be taught to look after and care for them By appreciating the value of trees, young people will learn to respect them more and, therefore, not want to destroy them.

It is, therefore, clear that individuals have as much a part to play as larger organisations in preserving woodlands and forests.

Word Count: 298

Possible Band: 7

Test 9 Task 1

The graph illustrates the actual and estimated visitors to a new art gallery between 1990 and 2001 and the pie charts give their satisfaction rating of the gallery in two years 1990 and 2001.

It was estimated that visitor numbers would be just under 500,000 in the first year rising gradually to double that number by the end of the period. While there were some fluctuations in the actual number of people visiting the gallery, attendances more than doubled from 1.5 million to just under 3.5 million in 2001.

Visitor numbers were influenced by three events during the period. In 1991, the director of the gallery was sacked with numbers dropping from approximately 2.25 million in 1991 to under 2 million the following year. By 1994 numbers had dropped to their 1990 level, when they started to rise. In 1995, when a new shop opened, numbers had gone up to almost 2.5 million. By the time the new director was appointed in 1995, numbers had reached 3 million. After that they slipped back, but then rose again.

The pie charts show that the *Satisfaction rating* for the gallery increased from 30% to 70% between 1990 and 2001.

It is clear from the graph that the actual number of people who visited the gallery exceeded expectations by a wide margin.

Word Count: 219

Possible Band: 7

Test 10 Task 1 Version 1

The graph shows the satisfaction rating of the staff in four colleges from 1991 to 2002

Of the four institutions only one, College C, improved its rating significantly over the period from just below 29%, the lowest rating, in 1991 to 80%, the highest rating, in 2002. Between 1991 and 1995, the rating for College C hovered below the 30% level, falling to a low of just over 10% in 1998. In 1999, the rating rocketed to just under 70%, rising gradually thereafter to finish the period at 80%.

The satisfaction trend for College B over the period fluctuated, but was still upward, climbing from just over 50% in 1991 to 70% in 2002. College A, by contrast, showed a gradual decline over the period from a 60% satisfaction rating in 1991 to 40% in 2002. Similarly, the fourth institution, College D's rating after hovering around the 40% level until 1997, declined gradually to 20% by 2002.

Word Count: 156.

Possible Band: 7

Test 10 Task 1 Version 2

The graph shows the satisfaction rating of the staff in four colleges, College A, College B, College C and College D from 1991 to 2002.

Only one college, College C, increased its rating over the period from about 29%, which was the lowest rating in 1991 to 80%, which was the highest rating, in 2002. Between 1991 and 1995, the rating for College C stayed below 30% and fell to a low of just 10% in 1998. In 1999, the rating of College C rose to just under 70%, and it rose gradually to 80% in 2002.

The satisfaction rating for College B over the period went up and down. It was still upward. It climbed from just over 50% in 1991 to 70% in 2002. College A went down gradually over the period from 60% in 1991 to 40% in 2002. The fourth institution, College D, stayed around 40% until 1997, and then it went down gradually to 20% by 2002.

Word Count: 162.

Possible Band: 6

Test 10 Task 1 Version 3

The graph show the satisfaction rating of the staff in four colleges, College A, College B, College C and College D from 1991 to 2002.

One college, College C, increased rating over period from about 29%, which was lowest rating in 1991 to 80%, which was highest rating, in 2002. Between 1991 to 1995, rating for College C stay below 30% and fell to low of just 10 in 1998. In 1999, the rating of College C rised to just under 70%, and it rised gradualy to 80% in 2002.

Satisfaction rating for College B over the period go up and down. It was still upward. It climb from just over 50% in 1991 to 70% in 2002. College A fell down gradually from 60% at 1991 to 40% at 2002. The fourth college, College D, stay around 40% until 1997, and then it go down gradually to 20% by 2002.

Word Count: 151.

Possible Band: 5

Note that this version contains mistakes. Can you find them?

It is better for you to use these sample answers as standards against which to measure your own writing. It is pointless learning them by heart and then trying to fit parts of them into answers in the exam.

Appendix

International English Language Testing System

 UNIVERSITY *of* CAMBRIDGE
Local Examinations Syndicate

 The British Council

 IDP Education Australia:
IELTS Australia

WRITING ANSWER SHEET

Candidate Name: ....   Candidate Number: ....

Centre Name: ....   Date: ....

Module: ACADEMIC   ☐   (Tick as appropriate)

         GENERAL TRAINING   ☐   Version: ....

TASK 1

_____

_____

_____

_____

_____

_____

_____

_____

_____

_____

_____

| EXAMINER'S USE ONLY |

EXAMINER 2 NUMBER: ....

CANDIDATE NUMBER: ....   EXAMINER 1 NUMBER: ....

SAMPLE

EXAMINER'S USE ONLY

EXAMINER 2
TASK 1

TF		CC		VSS		TOTAL	

GLOBAL BAND

EXAMINER 1
TASK 1

TF		CC		VSS		TOTAL	

GLOBAL BAND

Reproduced by permission of the University of Cambridge Local Examinations Syndicate